Acknowledgements

To my husband without whose help, encouragement and incisive advice nothing would have been achieved; to my daughters, Penelope and Alexandra, whose complete faith that I could finish the book spurred me on; to my publisher, Nick Bliss, whose constant encouragement was exceeded only by his endless patience; to David Sherborne of 5 Raymond Buildings for his penetrating legal comments; to my editor Evelyn Reid and finally to my Personal Assistant, Miss Samantha Lee, without whose skill in fashioning the drafts into a final manuscript, the book would not have been completed.

Contents

Table of Cases

Table of Statutes

Table of Statutory Instruments

Table of European Legislation

Introduction

Scope of the book

This book is intended for all who have an interest in the law of defamation as well as general practitioners who may need specialised information when giving advice on defamation. If one is defamed or accused of having made a defamatory statement it can be, to someone who is unfamiliar to it, a frightening and daunting experience. This practical guide is designed to reduce the mystique which commonly surrounds defamation and to set out clearly all the information needed for a person involved in libel proceedings. The book is intended to be referred to by anyone implicated in a defamation action, which may well be outside their experience, to establish firstly, whether the defamation is actionable and secondly, what the procedures are for bringing or defending a defamation action. Practical considerations for both parties to an action, the Plaintiff and Defendant, and those advising them, are also examined.

Importance of defamation law

From the way libel actions are reported, one might be forgiven for thinking that libel litigation was a branch of the entertainment industry. The high 'telephone number awards' sometimes made are considered by many to be almost obscene in relation to the damages for personal injury. Auberon Waugh has claimed that 'the purpose of libel laws is to protect rich crooks, politicians, people in authority and vain millionaires'. Although, as with any law, there will be abuses either by a gagging writ or by awards which may seem to be more of a lottery than a measured application of this branch of the law, it is essential in a free society that there should be a strong and effective defamation law.

The importance of protecting one's reputation against unwarranted attacks or in turn being able to refute an unfounded allegation of defaming somebody cannot be over-emphasised in this day of increasing media penetration. The multimedia technological age in which we live means that a chance remark uttered in a television programme can be beamed round the world within a matter of seconds, or a statement on the Internet World Wide Web can be accessed by millions of people. Once in a cuttings or reference library or database the statement or comment can be resurrected indefinitely. Equally in an age where sophisticated corruption is increasing, whether financial or political, it is imperative that investigative journalism should be free from unwarranted gagging writs.

For a person defamed, whether a well-known pop star, political figure or a private person trying to run a business, a defamatory and untrue statement can have disastrous consequences. An MP may be forced to resign, a pop star may have contracts cancelled, or a private individual may suffer financially, lose his job and be socially ostracised. This book is a stage-by-stage guide for all practitioners who may have clients in such a situation and need assistance in commencing proceedings to protect their reputation in this specialised arm of the law.

Similarly the journalist, broadcaster or author who receives a writ for defamation will require prompt and clear assistance as to how to defend a libel action. At the time of writing, there is no legal aid for defamation and therefore for most individuals involved in libel proceedings, whether as plaintiff or defendant, the financial consequences can be serious. This, combined with the implications of taking the matter to court with the almost inevitable result that there will be far wider publicity than that given to the original alleged libel, means that legal advice should be obtained promptly by either party to threatened libel proceedings.

This is a guide intended both for the general practitioner needing a simple but comprehensive guide to defamation and an *aide-mémoire* for more experienced legal practitioners and in-house lawyers connected with newspapers, magazines, books, TV and media.

Historically a civil remedy to protect reputation has been enshrined in the law since the earliest time and was probably given its most memorable expression in Shakespeare's lines from *Othello*:

> Who steals my purse steals trash;
> 'tis something, nothing; ...
> But he that filches from me my good name
> Robs me of that which not enriches him,
> and makes me poor indeed.

Defamation is an area of the law of tort which has developed its own complex and arcane system of pleadings. Libel is one branch of the law of defamation and slander is the other.

Definition of defamation

Libel is defamation in a permanent and visible form whereas slander is defamation by spoken words or in any ephemeral form, which can include disparaging gestures or actions. Libel includes not only writing or printing but also films, video tapes, cassettes, faxes, electronic mail and the Internet. Under s 1 of the Defamation Act 1952 and the Theatres Act 1968, radio and television broadcasts and theatre performances are all 'permanent forms'.

The purpose of the law of defamation is to protect the reputation of an individual from unjustified attack and the present law is codified in the Defamation Act 1952 and Defamation Act 1996. This book is concerned with the law of defamation in England and Wales. The law in Northern Ireland is govened by the Defamation Act (Northern Ireland) 1955 which is identical to the Defamation Act 1952. The majority of the 1996 Defamation Act applies to Northern Ireland but specific reference to it should be made as required. In relation to Scotland, there are more substantive differences, particularly in that no distinction is made between libel and slander but the majority of the sections of the 1996 Defamation Act extend to Scotland.

Layout of the book

This book will examine the law of defamation from the point of view of both a plaintiff, the person bringing the libel action, and a defendant, the person being sued. The practitioner will be guided through the way the law of defamation works in practice with each relevant step in a libel action explained. It will deal with the Defamation Act 1996 and its likely effect and it will examine recent developments in the field of libel, including the impact of European law and Internet libel and appeals. It will also give general advice in relation to both pre-publication steps as well as the procedures in a libel action.

A libel action is a form of litigation so that while normal rules, tactics and strategy for prosecuting or defending such litigation successfully can be adopted, defamation does involve its own particular and peculiar practices. This book is intended as a guide to both the individual who may find himself involved in libel proceedings and the general practitioner who wish to give preliminary advice in this specialised field. The traditionally recommended books are *Gatley on Libel and Slander*, *Carter-Ruck on Libel and Slander* and *Duncan and Neill on Defamation*. A number of libel cases referred to in the text are not reported in the

Law Reports and every effort has been made to provide as full a citation as possible.

The book is divided into five sections so that the reader can refer immediately to the particular area required.

Section I—The plaintiff
This covers those matters which a plaintiff has to establish to succeed in a libel action; Chapter 1 deals with the definition of defamation; Chapter 2 deals with identification and publication.

Section II—The defendant
This covers the principal defences; Chapters 3 and 4 explain justification and fair comment, Chapter 5 absolute and qualified privilege, Chapter 6 unintentional defamation and Chapter 7 other defences, such as consent, accord and satisfaction.

Section III—Related actions and relief available to plaintiffs
This covers those areas where a person feels his reputation has been damaged but for whatever reason recourse is not available to him through bringing a libel action. Chapter 8 examines criminal libel, malicious falsehood, blasphemy, slander of title, slander of goods and false attribution of authorship, Chapter 9 examines the relief available in libel proceedings.

Section IV—Proceedings
This takes the reader through each stage of a libel action from letters before action to the trial with particular emphasis on those areas of procedure pertaining to defamation. Chapter 10 examines all the pleadings with precedents.

Section V—Recent developments and general advice
This covers libel reform and general advice. Chapter 11 examines the new Defamation Act 1996; the impact of Europe; Internet libel and appeals. Chapter 12 considers general advice, libel avoidance and pre-publication advice, tactics and strategies in a libel action.

Appendix A
This sets out a list of significant libel damages awarded in libel actions from 1986 to 1996.

Appendix B
Defamation Act 1952 and Schedule.

Appendix C
Defamation Act 1996 and Schedule.

Appendix D
Chart of highest and lowest libel damages awards in each year from 1986 to 1996.

For easy reference Chapters 1–9 conclude with a check list.

Section I

The Plaintiff

In this section those matters which a plaintiff has to establish are considered as follows:

Chapter 1—Defamatory Statement

A defamatory statement
    Natural and ordinary meaning
    Rumour
    Innuendo
    Context
    Intent
    Ambiguous meaning
    Slander
    Damages
    Trial procedure

Chapter 2—Identification

Identification of the plaintiff
    Plaintiff named
    Plaintiff innocently named
    Plaintiff not named
    Class of persons
    Company, county council, trade union, partnership
    Burden of proof
Publication
    Publication to a third person
    Foreign publication
    Who to sue
    Initial steps

Chapter 1

Defamatory Statement

While the public perception may be that a successful plaintiff in a libel action is commonly awarded huge sums for little effort, it is important to remember that not all the burden in a libel action falls upon a defendant. The plaintiff in a libel action has to establish three matters to the satisfaction of the judge and jury (if any) and each of these will be considered in turn. The three matters which a plaintiff has to establish on the balance of probabilities are that:

(a) the words of which complaint is made are defamatory;

(b) those words have been understood to refer to him; and

(c) there has been publication to a third party.

A plaintiff who issues a writ for libel may have many reasons for doing so. He may wish to:

(a) prevent the further dissemination of the defamatory material;

(b) prevent publication altogether if he becomes aware of the defamatory statement before publication;

(c) preserve his position but may be content with an immediate apology;

(d) stifle discussion about a particular area, the so called gagging writ;

(e) issue the writ on a technicality because he will require a statement in open court; or

(f) obtain damages.

Whatever the motive the plaintiff may have in issuing the writ, those advising him should check that the basic elements to substantiate such an action, as set out above, are in place.

A defamatory statement

To advise the client whether or not the matter of which he complains can be pursued through the courts, it is necessary to establish whether the statement is defamatory. This is a question of fact in each case. In deciding and advising there are three judicial statements which are widely regarded as the leading definitions. The first and perhaps the most well known is the ruling by Parke J in *Parmiter v Coupland* (1840) 6 M & W p 105:

> A statement concerning any person which exposes him to hatred, ridicule or contempt or which causes him to be shunned or avoided or which has a tendency to injure him in his office, profession or trade.

The second judicial definition of what constitutes a defamatory statement is by Cave J in *Scott v Sampson* (1882) 8 QBD 491:

> ... a false statement about a man to his discredit.

The final definition which is often quoted, is by Lord Aitken in *Sim v Stretch* (1936) 52 TLR 669:

> ... words which tend to lower the person in the estimation of right-thinking members of society.

In examining a statement to see whether it is defamatory it is necessary to be clear about its meaning: are the words in their natural and ordinary meaning defamatory or is the defamatory meaning hidden in innuendo? Each of these is examined below. The falsity of the statement does not have to be proved by the plaintiff, but its defamatory nature does.

Natural and ordinary meaning

A statement that a man is a thief or a murderer is clearly defamatory. Obviously in deciding whether or not words are defamatory and whether they would offend 'right-thinking members of society' regard must be had to the morality prevailing at the time. For example, in the time of Charles II, it was defamatory to state that a person was a papist and went to mass. In 1926, it was held defamatory to say that a man was a communist.

Examples

Examples of words which have been held to be defamatory in recent years are the businessman, Tobias, wrongly accused of repackaging and selling food past its sell by date, who recovered damages of £470,000 (with two other plaintiffs) against the *Mail on Sunday* in July 1989; the two sisters, Chastell and Warby, who were awarded damages of £7,500 each against Tesco in 1989 on appeal over an allegation that they had tried to cheat the store of £2 by switching price labels; a fisherman,

Maddocks, who was accused of faking an angling contest and recovered £150,00 damages against *Angling Mail* in May 1989; a WPC, Trebith, who was accused of unseemly behaviour recovered damages of £60,000 against the *Sunday Sport* in December 1989; a Mrs Winyard and her son recovered damages of £75,000 and £15,000 respectively against the *Tatler* in July 1990 for an article criticising the way in which they ran their health farm and a caravan park owner, Johnson, who was accused of misrepresenting his holidays in France was awarded £350,000 damages against Radio City in November 1970. These statements which involve people who did not have a high profile were all held to be defamatory.

Higher profile plaintiffs where the words were held to be defamatory were *Coronation Street* actor, Bill Roache, who recovered £50,000 damages against the *Sun* newspaper in November 1991 for a statement that he was boring, boastful, and disliked by his fellow actors; the actor, Jason Connery, who recovered £35,000 damages, also against the *Sun* in January 1992, for a statement that he had been cowardly and would rather have killed himself than fight in the Gulf War; the pop star, Jason Donovan, who recovered £200,000 damages in April 1992 against the pop magazine *The Face* over a statement that implied he was homosexual and hypocritical.

In October 1995, several cricketers of West Indian origin won damages against *Wisden Cricket Monthly* ((1995), unreported) over an article entitled 'Is it in the blood?' which suggested that players of West Indian, Asian or South African origin would be motivated more by desires of personal advancement or achievement than by national pride. Philip de Freitas won damages estimated at £50,000 while Devon Malcolm accepted in settlement what were described as 'substantial' damages.

In considering natural and ordinary meanings it is important to consider also the reasonable inferences that can be drawn from those meanings. In *Lewis v Daily Telegraph Ltd* [1964] AC 234, a front page article under the headline 'Fraud squad probe firm' reported that the City Fraud Squad were enquiring into the affairs of the Rubber Improvement Company and the article went on to name the chairman as Mr John Lewis. The company and Mr Lewis sued alleging that the article bore the defamatory meaning that their affairs were conducted fraudulently or dishonestly. It was held by the House of Lords that the words were defamatory and although they were not capable of meaning that the plaintiffs were guilty of fraud they could mean that the plaintiffs were suspected of fraud. Substantial damages were awarded, although these were later reduced on appeal.

The singer Elton John famously recovered £350,000 against the *Sunday Mirror* in 1993 over a statement that he had an eating disorder and had been seen regurgitating crisps at a Hollywood party. In the same year the television personality Esther Rantzen was awarded £250,000 against the *People* over a statement that she had concealed evidence relating to a person involved in her Childline Charity. The footballer, Graeme Souness, was awarded £750,000 in 1995 against the *Daily Mirror* for a statement that he behaved badly to his ex-wife over their divorce. A number of these decisions were reduced on appeal and will be dealt with in Section V, Chapter 11.

The well-known explorer, Sir Ranulph Twistleton-Fiennes, recovered £100,000 damages, in 1990, against a magazine for a statement that his many explorations were of no scientific or historical value and (although the amount was later reduced before appeal) the jury found that this was a statement to his discredit. A six-year-old plaintiff, Jonathan Hunt, sued the *Sun* newspaper through his mother in May 1991 over a statement that he was 'the worst brat in Britain' and damages of £35,000 were awarded. In 1990, libel proceedings were started over a letter purporting to come from the plaintiff, David Prendergast, President of the breakaway Union of Democratic Miners. It was a forged letter which the plaintiff alleged had been produced from 'somewhere within the NUM' and appeared to have been written by him suggesting that he was betraying members of the NUM in the Nottingham area. It was held to be to his discredit and he recovered £100,000 damages.

In July 1991 the Tory MP, Teresa Gorman, was the victim of a mock press release circulated in her name to her fellow MPs by her constituency chairman. The press release, which followed a dispute between her and the chairman, pointed to her lack of charm and mocked the hormone replacement therapy she was receiving. This was held to be defamatory and she recovered £150,000 damages, reduced on appeal in October 1992 to £50,000.

Rumour

Where a statement is made where the defamatory allegation is only a rumour and has been denied, the plaintiff can still recover damages.

Examples

In 1993, the Prime Minister, John Major, sued the *New Statesman* and the magazine *Scallywag* for libel over an article purporting to examine the falsities of rumours being spread about him and the Downing Street cook Miss Clare Latimer. The article made it clear that the rumours were totally untrue, but libel damages were paid by distributors of the alleged libel to the Prime Minister and Miss Latimer.

In *Aspro Travel Ltd v Owners Abroad Group plc* [1996] 1 WLR 132, CA a travel firm Aspro Travel Ltd sued a rival travel firm Owners Abroad Group plc. Representatives of Owners Abroad had claimed to hotel owners and travel agents in Cyprus that Aspro Travel were going bankrupt. The plaintiffs sued for libel and the defendants sought to justify that there had been reasonable grounds to suspect that the plaintiffs' commercial viability was weak but did not seek to justify that the company was insolvent; they also pleaded qualified privilege. It was held that there could be circumstances in which a rumour could be repeated, even before it was established that the rumour was true. As the point was at least arguable, the defence of justification was not struck out.

A statement may be defamatory whether or not it is true. If it is true, there may be a defence of justification (Section II, Chapter 3). Conversely, an untrue statement may not be defamatory although it may be actionable on other grounds (Section III, Chapter 8).

Innuendo

The above examples of defamatory statements are relatively obvious where the words in what is described as their natural and ordinary meaning are clearly those where right-thinking members of society would think less of the person described. There may however be statements which in their natural and ordinary meaning are innocuous but because of certain circumstances known to those to whom the statements were made, they reflect adversely upon the plaintiff. In those circumstances, the words are described as defamatory by innuendo.

Examples

One of the earliest cases concerning a defamatory innuendo was the case of *Russell v Notcutt* (1896) 12 TLR 195, CA which involved a poster announcing that the plaintiff would be singing at a concert. The plaintiff, a well-known concert singer, complained that the poster advertising the concert showed her name in the middle of the list of attractions not at the beginning or the end. She was able to show that the best singer was normally first or last and placing her name in the middle of the list could be defamatory of her. Another classic libel case on innuendo was the case of *Tolley v Fry* [1931] AC 333. In this case a photograph of a well-known amateur golfer was published showing him with a bar of Fry's chocolate protruding from his pocket. He sued for defamation on the grounds that the photograph, taken without his consent or knowledge, implied that he was receiving money for advertising. He recovered libel damages. More recently, an unmarried girl was portrayed as pregnant when an artist's impression was done of her and featured in a Kellogs advertising campaign under the caption 'A pregnant mum doesn't have to be constipated'. The girl, who was not pregnant, successfully sued the advertising agency for libel.

A celebrated example was the case of the former leader of the Labour Party then in opposition, the Right Honourable Michael Foot MP. In 1978, the *Daily Mail* reported that he had obtained private hospital treatment. Mr Foot instituted proceedings for libel and claimed that the article by innuendo meant that he was hypocritical and insincere in his well-known advocacy of egalitarianism. In addition, he was able to show that he had specifically requested that he should be placed in a public ward. He recovered libel damages.

The American piano entertainer, Liberace, recovered £8,000 damages from the *Daily Mirror* in 1959 for an article implying homosexuality which had described him as 'this deadly, winking, sniggering, snuggling chromium-plated scent-impregnated, luminous, quivering, giggling, fruit-flavoured, mincing, ice-covered heap of mother love'.

In 1986, Lord Gowrie recovered 'substantial' damages over an article in the *Star* newspaper which implied that he took drugs. Lord Gowrie had resigned as a minister and considerable publicity was given to the fact that his reason for his resignation was that he could not bring up his family on his ministerial salary of £33,000 a year. Under the headline 'A lordly price to pay' the article stated:

> There has been much excited chatter as to why dashing poetry-scribbling minister, Lord Gowrie, left the Cabinet so suddenly. What expensive habits can he not support on an income of £33,000? I am sure Gowrie himself would snort at the suggestion that he was born with a silver spoon round his neck.

Lord Gowrie's counsel stated on his behalf that there were those who were aware that the reference to the word 'snort' and a 'silver spoon round the neck' carried the implication that the plaintiff had taken drugs.

Innuendo was also the basis of a successful libel action by a travel firm who recovered damages from the BBC when a programme criticising it for a somewhat dictatorial holiday villa regime on the Costa del Sol was accentuated by the opening theme music from the *Colditz Story*, a television series about the prisoner of war camp.

An action by singer Dorothy Squires then married to the actor Roger Moore against the *News of the World* in 1971 concerning an article under the headline 'How my love for the Saint went sour' also relied on innuendo. She claimed that the article as published bore the innuendo that she was a woman ready to wash her dirty linen in public for money. She had not in fact received any payment, denied making the statements attributed to her and recovered damages against the *News of the World*. This is to be compared with the case in 1985 where MP, Jonathan Aitken, wrote a light-hearted article for his local paper comparing his local MP's wife to Sue Ellen of the American TV soap opera *Dallas*. She sued for libel alleging that by innuendo, this meant that she had similar problems to the fictional character and that she was therefore portrayed as an alcoholic prostitute. The article was not held to be capable of being understood by the reasonable reader to mean this and she lost her action. (See also Section II, Chapter 7.)

Context

Both the plaintiff and the defendant are entitled to plead that the alleged defamatory words should be considered in the context of other words in the publication complained of. For example, in a book the plaintiff may refer to other parts of the book as well as the defamatory statement, and may refer to other passages which may render the statement more defamatory. Similarly, a defendant may in his defence plead other words not complained about by the plaintiff which may mitigate or contradict the alleged defamatory meaning. The circumstances in which the alleged defamatory statement came to be made can also be relevant, for example, in a conversation with a reporter defamatory statements may be put to a future plaintiff and it could be relevant that he may fail to deny such statements.

Examples

Two contrasting interlocutory decisions on context were decided in 1995. In the first, two actors from the television series, *Neighbours*, sued the *News of the World*. The *News of the World* had published a report of a pornographic computer game which had been made with the two actors' faces superimposed on the bodies involved with a photograph under the headline 'Strewth! What's Harold up to with our Madge?'. The article made it quite clear that the actors had known nothing about their faces being superimposed in the pornographic game. The case went to the Court of Appeal and eventually the House of Lords held that the plaintiffs could not take the headline or the photographs in isolation; when considered as a whole the article was not defamatory.

An interesting contrast was provided by a Court of Appeal decision later in the same year. In *Gillick v BBC* (1995) *The Times*, 20 October,

CA the well-known anti-abortion campaigner, Victoria Gillick, sued the BBC over a statement on a television broadcast concerning the rise in teenage pregnancies. The facts were that Mrs Gillick had sought to have withdrawn a circular giving general practitioners the right to give contraceptive advice to underage girls without their parents' consent. Although her action to withdraw the circular failed in the House of Lords, she claimed on the programme that in the two years before the House of Lords overruled her previously successful application in 1985, the number of teenage pregnancies had declined. A journalist on the programme retorted that 'there were at least two reported cases of suicide by girls who were pregnant after 1984'. Mrs Gillick sued for libel and it was held that within the context of a serious discussion on a grave subject, these words were capable of meaning that she was morally responsible for those deaths and that the words would not simply have been understood as a coincidental or flippant remark.

In *Telnikoff v Matusevitch* [1991] 3 WLR 952 an article in the *Daily Telegraph* gave rise to a letter which formed the subject matter of libel proceedings. The defendant, the writer of the letter, failed in the attempt to have the article, as well as the letter which followed it, considered at the same time by the jury. It was held that the letter should be considered on its own and the article could not be part of the context. (See also Section II, Chapter 4.)

Intent

The defendant's intention in making the statement is irrelevant. The defendant may not have intended to refer to the plaintiff, may have believed the words to be true, or may have made them in jest or accidentally or without being aware of circumstances where they could be understood to refer to the plaintiff, but if the words are held to be defamatory and there is no defence, then the defendant's intent will only count in mitigation. Conversely, even if the defendant intends to make a defamatory statement, if it is held not to be defamatory, then the plaintiff cannot succeed. The only exceptions to the irrelevance of the defendant's intention are the technical defences of innocent defamation and malice (see Section II, Chapter 6).

Examples

The leading case on intent is *Hulton v Jones* [1910] AC 20. The *Sunday Chronicle* as it then was, published an article by their foreign correspondent describing the scenes at the motor racing at Dieppe. The account was entirely fictitious although written as fact. Part of the article read:

There is Artemus Jones with a woman who is not his wife, who must be, you know, the other thing. Really is it not surprising how certain of our fellow countrymen behave when they come abroad? Who would suppose by his goings on that he was a church warden at Peckham?

The name was made up and the account was completely fictitious but unfortunately there was at that time a barrister practising on the North Wales circuit, Thomas Artemus Jones, known by some of his friends as Artemus Jones. He had, for some time, been a contributor of articles to that particular newspaper and it was held that intention was irrelevant, the article purported to be an account of a factual event, evidence was given that it had been understood to refer to the plaintiff and he recovered damages.

A television company broadcasting a news programme accidentally included a comment made by a bystander which was defamatory of the local MP. This was broadcast as part of the news bulletin and the MP recovered damages, although the television company had no intention of defaming him. However, under s 1 of the Defamation Act 1996 there is a provision limiting responsibility for publication to those primarily responsible which includes the author, editor and publisher. It is possible therefore that in a case such as this, there might be a defence under s 1 (see Section II, Chapter 6).

Another case involved publication of a photograph of a man and a woman captioned 'Mr X and his fiancee' (*Cassidy v Daily Mirror* [1929] 2 KB 331). Unfortunately, unknown to the newspaper, Mr X was already married and his wife succeeded in a libel action. The caption was held to be capable of the defamatory innuendo that she was unlawfully married to Mr X, and she was awarded £500 damages.

Even the publication of an apology, where it is clearly not intended that there should be a defamation, can still be defamatory. In *Tracy v Kemsley Newspapers Ltd* (1954), unreported, an apology was published by the *Sunday Times* without the journalist's consent. The journalist sued after publication of the apology and claimed that the apology implied that she was an irresponsible journalist who had been careless. She was awarded damages. In *Watts v Times Newspapers* (1995) *The Times*, 22 September a similar situation arose. In that case, an article in *The Times* had accused an author, Watts, of plagiarism but inadvertently had accompanied the article with a photograph of Watts, a property developer. *The Times* published an apology to Watts, the property developer, and Watts, the author, sued for libel over the wording of the apology which repeated the accusation of plagiarism against him. (See Section II, Chapter 5.)

Ambiguous meaning

Where a plaintiff seeks to rely on a defamatory innuendo where the words may be either innocent or equivocal, such as 'fruit-flavoured' in the Liberace case implying homosexuality, or a case involving the late Kenneth Tynan where he was stated to be 'preoccupied with the bent', the plaintiff has to specify, as will be seen in Section IV, Chapter 10, precisely the defamatory meaning or meanings which he alleges the words can be understood to bear. In the Kenneth Tynan case, he stated that the words 'preoccupied by the bent' meant by innuendo either that he was a homosexual or that he was a criminal.

Example

In 1992 the pop star Jason Donovan sued *The Face* magazine which had featured a photograph of him wearing a T-shirt with the caption 'Queer as f***'. Mr Donovan alleged that the article insinuated that he was a liar and a hypocrite for maintaining that he was heterosexual. The magazine denied that the photograph which they claimed was obviously a mock-up could bear that meaning. Jason Donovan gave evidence that he was not homosexual and the jury accepted that the photograph could have that meaning and awarded him £200,000 damages.

Slander

The test of what is defamatory in relation to slander is the same for libel, except that there can also be slander by gesture or action. The important distinction in the case of libel is that damage is presumed whereas in the case of slander, damage must be proved with the exception of the circumstances set out in s 2 of the Defamation Act 1952. This provides that the damage does not have to be proved in a slander action:

(a) where the words impute a crime for which the plaintiff could be imprisoned;

(b) where the words are calculated to disparage the plaintiff in any office trade, business or profession or calling held at the time;

(c) where the words impute to the plaintiff a contagious or infectious disease; and

(d) where the words impute adultery or unchastity to a woman or girl (Slander of Women Act 1891).

In this age of increasing electronic communication, radio, television and satellite broadcasting will be treated as libel rather than slander. Video is also treated as libel but the question remains undecided as to whether a defamatory statement on the Internet falls under libel or slander although being more than transitory or ephemeral it is likely that it would be treated as libel. Any proceedings alleging a defamatory statement on the Internet should plead libel and slander.

Examples

In *Smith v Houston* (1991), unreported, Dr Smith sued a fellow lady doctor, Dr Houston, who shared his surgery but was no longer his partner. Dr Houston, the defendant, was alleged to have shouted, within earshot of staff and patients, remarks which stated clearly that Dr Smith was sexually harassing nurses. He was awarded £150,000 damages although this was later reduced on appeal (see Section V, Chapter 11).Dr Smith's action was only the sixth reported slander action in the preceding 20 years. In June 1994, a millionaire, Mr Wraith, sued his ex-wife for slander when she claimed that he had given her a sexually transmitted disease. The jury heard evidence that he frequented brothels and awarded him damages of £69, the price of a bottle of champagne at the Dutch sex club the husband had frequented.

In 1983, Robert Mason, landlord of a pub in central London successfully sued William Hill the Bookmakers who had frogmarched him out of a betting shop. He sued on the defamatory innuendo that this action meant he was a person who could not settle his debts. He recovered £44,000 damages. A woman falsely arrested for shoplifting by a store detective in the street recovered damages for slander on the basis that the action of arresting her implied that she was guilty.

Damages

As has been seen, the plaintiff in a libel action, in contrast to a slander action, does not have to prove damage. The categories of damages which can be awarded for a plaintiff are set out in Section III, Chapter 9. While it is generally true that the motives, conduct and intention of the defendant are irrelevant, apart from the question of malice (see Section II, Chapters 4 and 5), the defendant's behaviour can be taken into account in assessing damages, including the conduct of the defendant from the date when the matter was first drawn to his attention, up to and including his conduct of the defendant and his advisers during the trial. The jury is entitled to consider hurt feelings of the plaintiff but no such damages for wounded pride or feelings may be awarded against a corporate plaintiff, since a company can only be injured in its pocket.

Trial procedure

At the trial of a libel action a judge rules whether or not the words complained of are capable of a defamatory meaning, while the jury decides whether the words were in fact defamatory and if so whether the pleaded defences are successful or not. If not the jury alone decides the amount of any damages. A jury is automatic in a libel action unless the case is one of great technical complexity (see Section I, Chapter 2), where it will be heard by a judge alone.

Check list

(1) Are the words defamatory, either on the face of them or by innu-endo?

(2) If the words are not defamatory on their face, what are the facts which your client relies on to show that the words are defamatory?

(3) What exactly were the circumstances of publication?

(4) Was he approached before publication for his comments?

(5) What was he told about the proposed publication? (These factors are relevant to malice.)

(6) Is the plaintiff prepared for the financial consequences of taking the matter to trial?

(7) Is the plaintiff prepared to see the alleged libel given far wider publicity if the matter goes to trial and is repeated by the press?

(8) Does the plaintiff appreciate that even if he wins and recovers damages, he will only recover approximately two-thirds of his costs?

Chapter 2

Identification

Identification of the plaintiff

The second matter which a plaintiff has to establish is that the words have been understood to refer to him. Obviously where the plaintiff is named this can be established without difficulty. Where the plaintiff is not named however, provided he can produce evidence to show that people who had read the words had understood them to refer to him, he can establish identification

Plaintiff named

Where the plaintiff is named then there is no difficulty in showing that the words were understood to refer to him.

Example
The headline 'You Dirty Rat' above an article criticising the way Graeme Souness had treated his ex-wife over their divorce enabled the footballer to recover libel damages of £750,000 when he successfully sued the *Daily Mirror* in 1995 (*Souness v MGN* (1995), unreported).

Plaintiff innocently named

In certain cases the name of a plaintiff will be published quite innocently, either because of a mistake or because the name has been made up.

Examples
In the case of *Newstead v London Express* [1940] 1 KB 377, a newspaper in reporting bigamy proceedings stated that 'Harold Newstead, 30-year-old Camberwell man, who was jailed for nine months, liked having

two wives at a time'. Unknown to the newspaper, there were two Harold Newsteads and the innocent one, who also lived in Camberwell, recovered libel damages.

In the 1970s, *The Times* published an article about the financial ruin of a gambler and former owner of Harrods, Hugh Fraser. Accompanying the article was a photograph of the highly respected Tory MP, Sir Hugh Fraser, who obtained damages of £10,000.

One of the leading cases on the innocent naming of a defendant is *Hulton v Jones* [1910] AC 20 (see Chapter 1). As has been seen the name of Artemus Jones was completely made up, it was a fictitious account, but not withstanding that it was held that it could be defamatory of the real Artemus Jones.

There is now a limited defence where there has been an innocent mistake—s 4 of the Defamation Act 1952 and now ss 2–4 of the Defamation Act 1996 (see Section II, Chapter 6).

Plaintiff not named

If a plaintiff can show that the words have been understood to refer to him, even if he has not been named, then provided he can show that the statement had been published and is defamatory, he can recover damages.

Examples

In *Morgan v Odhams Press Ltd* [1971] 1 WLR 1239, the plaintiff was not named or referred to in the article complained of but recovered damages. This case involved a newspaper article which stated that a named woman had been 'kidnapped by members of a dog doping gang and kept in a house in Finchley'. The woman involved had stayed in the plaintiff's flat near Finchley for a number of days. Several people who had seen the woman in a distressed state with the plaintiff on various days during the period under discussion gave evidence that they had read the article and thought it referred to the plaintiff. The jury agreed and although the plaintiff was not named or referred to at all he was able to satisfy the judge and jury that he was identifiable. In another case, a novel featured a school secretary who was described as a 'dried up spinster' who sent poison pen letters in the story. A spinster who had been a school secretary issued proceedings for libel and it transpired that the author had worked at the same school as the plaintiff and had modelled the fictional character upon her. The matter was settled on terms which included the withdrawal and amendment of the book.

In 1980, Judge Doyle, a Catholic, recovered libel damages against

The Economist. It had published the following paragraph:

> When the three new county court judges were finally appointed last month one of them was in fact a Catholic. But his appointment has come in for criticism in the Bar Library in Belfast, particularly among Catholic QCs, who consider that he was appointed as a token, and that some of their Protestant colleagues would have been better fitted for the job.

The plaintiff was able to show that this referred to him as he had been identified because he was the only Catholic who had been appointed as a judge, and he recovered £50,000 damages. In 1978, the then leader of the Liberal Party, Jeremy Thorpe, was alleged to have been involved in a plot to kill a Mr Norman Scott. The *Daily Telegraph* reported that the name of 'a wealthy benefactor of the Liberal Party' had been given to the police in connection with the affair. The article alleged that the benefactor had been a member of the plot to kill Norman Scott. Jack Hayward, a millionaire who had contributed generously to the Liberal Party, sued for libel and evidence was given that readers had understood the words to refer to him. He denied absolutely any involvement in the so-called Norman Scott affair and was awarded £50,000 damages.

Another example occurred in a book where a well-known Lloyd's of London underwriter complained about a reference to him. There was a general comment about the heavy losses incurred on some reinsurance business and although the plaintiff was not referred to by name in that particular passage, he was referred to elsewhere in the book. He claimed that a reader looking at the passage referring to him by name would link this at a later stage with the passage commenting on the substantial losses. Had the matter proceeded to trial he would have had to produce evidence that a reader reading the book had indeed understood the second passage, where he was not mentioned, to refer to him.

Class of persons

Defamatory statements are frequently made in general terms such as, for example, 'all police officers', 'all lawyers', 'all journalists' or journalists working for a particular newspaper. In that situation it is a question of fact in each case as to whether the plaintiff can show that he has been clearly understood to be within that class because it is small and precisely defined enough.

Examples

The leading case is *Knupffer v London Express Newspapers* [1944] AC 116. In that case, a newspaper published an article from a foreign correspondent, commenting adversely on an association of certain Russian political refugees in terms which it was conceded would have been defamatory had they been made of an individual. The association numbered some 24 members in the UK and the plaintiff was active head of that branch. He sued for libel on the grounds that it reflected upon him personally but it was held that the article made allegations of a defamatory nature about a large body of persons throughout the world and it did not reflect on him personally.

A television programme investigating corruption and bribery in the police force started with a shot of a CID officer leaving a West End central police station at the same time as the voice-over was talking in general terms about CID men taking bribes. Apart from the clip, the programme did not identify or make any accusations against that officer but he sued for libel. The statement was held to reflect upon him and he recovered libel damages.

An article in the *Spectator* criticised court reporters on a famous trial and alleged that they were 'beer sodden hacks'. No names were given but about 12 reporters recovered damages because they were able to show that there were only a small number of reporters involved in that particular trial.

Another important case on defamation of a class of persons was in 1984 when the *News of the World* published a front page article with the headline 'Siege man tells us why he did it' *(Riches v News Group Newspapers Ltd* [1985] 2 All ER 845). It was reported that a man holding hostages at gun point claimed that policemen had raped and beaten his wife. No officers were named but Banbury CID was mentioned. There were only ten CID officers in the Banbury force and they sued and recovered damages.

Similarly, ten London police officers travelling in an unmarked van recovered damages against a television company who had broadcast an investigation into the beating up of three youths by officers from an unmarked police van. Two vans were in the area at the time and the ten officers in the van which was not involved sued and recovered damages. Another police officer class case involved the *Camden New Journal*, where eight police officers recovered agreed damages and costs over an article concerning the arrest of a black woman although none of the police officers were named.

In a work of fiction it can be more difficult for a plaintiff to establish identification. If, however, the work is set in a precise and real environment, such as in a thriller with police working at identifiable police stations or, for example, in a musical or theatrical milieu, then it may be possible for an unnamed plaintiff to recover damages. This also applies where an author has written an autobiographical book, in which despite the fact that all names may have been changed in the text, the mere fact that the book appears with the author's real name may mean that those referred to will be identifiable.

Examples

An author had lived for some time in a Cornish village. He then moved to another location but published a book which featured a short story concerning a number of people in a small Cornish village, who were depicted in unflattering terms. The work was clearly autobiographical and although names had been changed, a number of persons who lived in the real village successfully sued for libel.

An interesting example of the problems of class libel occurred in *Aiken v Police Review* (1995), unreported. The facts were that ten serving police officers sued for damages for libel over an article which appeared in the *Police Review* on 14 February 1992. As a preliminary issue, the defence pleaded that the plaintiffs would not have been identifiable. The article referred to a Metropolitan Police dog handler 'who recently won the right not to work on Saturdays because of his Jewish faith, is quitting the force amid claims of anti-semitism among colleagues'. The article, which was accompanied by a photograph of PC Brown, the Metropolitan dog handler, went on to refer to an example of anti-Semitism when a number of his colleagues starting singing the Nazi party anthem and giving the Nazi salute when he attended a Christmas party. The article also criticised senior officers who wanted him to leave. The plaintiffs, who were all long standing Metropolitan dog handlers, claimed that they were identifiable because they had served in the same dog handling section (one out of eight) within the Metropolitan Police. Interestingly enough, the plaintiffs sought to rely on a large number of articles in the national press which had given publicity to PC Brown's complaint. It was held that there were approximately 27 dog handlers who had served in the plaintiffs' section during the relevant period and that the ten plaintiffs were at least arguably capable of being identified from the article.

Company, county council, trade union, partnership

A company, as well as an individual, has a reputation which can be damaged, and although it cannot be awarded damages for hurt feelings or distress, it can be awarded damages for injury to its goodwill.

Examples

Imputations that a finance company was charging a true rate of interest of 160 per cent or harassing its tenants have been held to be defamatory.

In 1993, Anita and Gordon Roddick and the company they founded, the Body Shop, sued Channel Four over a television programme they alleged was defamatory because it questioned both their well-known commitment to animal-free testing and the sales methods of their staff. The plea of justification failed and libel damages were recovered by all three plaintiffs of £1,000 and in addition the Body Shop was awarded special damages for loss of profit of £273,000. In the same year, Richard Branson and his airline, Virgin Airways, received, in a widely publicised settlement, £500,000 to Richard Branson personally and £110,000 agreed damages to Virgin Airways for defamation from British Airways concerning allegations over 'dirty tricks'.

Bovril successfully sued a book publisher over an allegation that its product contained sugar, on the grounds that there was a defamatory innuendo that the company had lied about Bovril's contents. In 1995 it was announced that PowerGen, the privatised electricity generator, was to sue the *Observer* for defamation over allegations that six of its directors had cashed in £3.5m of share options in 1994, at a time when they were aware of a secret five-year forecast of deteriorating profits. In 1995, Woodgate Farms Dairy, which supplied Tesco, Sainsbury and Safeways supermarket chains with milk, issued a writ for libel against the *Observer*, as the paper had done an undercover investigation into a dairy which it claimed sold old recycled milk. The claim was subsequently settled.

An organisation can also sue. For example, in 1995, the Stock Exchange issued proceedings for defamation against the head of an Internet dealing venture called Sharelink. The Stock Exchange had refused to supply share prices to the new Internet-based dealing venture the day before the launch and a director of Sharelink had criticised the Stock Exchange resulting in the proceedings for defamation.

Recently, a firm of solicitors issued a libel writ against the Consumers Association following a damning report in the magazine *Which* about the quality and price of solicitors' services, naming five firms. The matter was later settled.

Liverpool Solicitors, Paul Rooney & Co, who acted for the boys accused of the murder of the child, James Bulger, sued Mirror Group Newspapers over a report in the *People* in 1993 criticising them. Under the headline 'James ... and why the lawyers are guilty too', the article implied that the lawyers had advised their clients to plead not guilty to increase fees and to appear on television. The *People* published an apology and the action was subsequently settled on payment of damages.

The fourth largest private medical insurers, Western Provident Association, also issued a writ for libel in 1995 against Norwich Union over the circulation of electronic messages suggesting that WPA was in financial trouble.

The chain store giant, Marks and Spencer, issued a writ in January 1996 against the makers of the television programme *World in Action* over claims that Marks and Spencer's suppliers in Morocco were using child labour. A libel action against the *News of the World* over a similar allegation was settled the same year with a statement in open court in which the allegations were withdrawn, the defendants apologised and paid a substantial donation to a charity.

The anti-fur pressure group, Lynx, was sued for libel in 1990 by a fur farm and the result of the proceedings was to bankrupt Lynx, which ceased campaigning.

It was held in the case of *Derbyshire County Council v Times Newspapers Ltd* [1993] 1 WLR 449 that a county council cannot itself sue for libel but individual councillors may. In that case, the *Sunday Times* had attacked the integrity of investment decisions made by Derbyshire County Council. Proceedings were issued by Derbyshire County Council, its leader, David Bookbinder, and the businessman Owen Oyston. While the newspaper paid damages to the two individuals, it successfully argued that the county council could not sue for libel.

This decision was followed in 1996 when a libel action brought by British Coal (formerly the National Coal Board) against the National Union of Mineworkers was halted. The action concerned criticisms made in the National Union of Mineworkers' magazine, *The Yorkshire Miner*, about British Coal's conduct in not making employers' contributions to the mineworkers' pension scheme. In contrast it is established, however, that a trade union may sue for libel.

Burden of proof

In all cases the onus is on the plaintiff to show that the person who read the alleged libel identified him and this is done by bringing witnesses forward who read the article to say that when they read it they believed that it referred to the plaintiff.

Example

In *Morgan v Odhams Press Ltd* [1971] 1 WLR 1239 (see Section I, Chapter 2, above) witnesses came forward to give evidence that when they had read the article complained of, they believed it referred to the plaintiff.

Publication

Publication to a third person

A plaintiff has to prove that there has been publication to a third person. Obviously in the case of radio, television, newspapers and books this is established without difficulty but publication to one person is sufficient to constitute publication for the purposes of libel. Similarly, if a letter containing defamatory statements is sent to the defamed person only, marked 'strictly private and confidential' in circumstances where only he will open it, then there has been no publication to a third party. There will be publication where in the ordinary course of events the letter will be opened by the defamed person's secretary. Sending a defamatory letter to an individual in an unsealed envelope, however, would require the plaintiff to produce evidence that persons other than himself had seen it.

A defamatory statement must be communicated to a third person and it has been held that if a defamatory postcard is sent, there can be presumption of publication to a third party. The extent of publication, however, may be relevant to the amount of any damages (see Section III, Chapter 9). Similarly, publication to a third party must not be by the plaintiff but by the defendant. If, therefore, the plaintiff receives a defamatory letter and shows it to a third party himself, the writer of the defamatory letter would not be liable for the publication.

Example

In *Lord Aldington v Tolstoy and Watts* (1989), unreported, some 10,000 copies of a pamphlet prepared by the two defendants were circulated in and around the Winchester area where the plaintiff lived, and to members of Parliament. The pamphlet alleged that Lord Aldington had been involved in the forcible repatriation of Cossack and Yugoslav prisoners of war to Russia at the end of the Second World War to their certain death. Although the libel had not been published in a mass circulation newspaper, record damages of £1.5m were awarded (see Section III, Chapter 9).

This case also aptly illustrates one of the hazards of taking a libel action to trial. As a result of the publicity which the six-week trial occasioned, the very serious allegations against Lord Aldington became front page news on every newspaper and a number of television bulletins for the duration of the trial. It is true, of course, that his public vindication by the award of such record damages was also headline news (see also Section III, Chapter 9).

Foreign publication

Where the alleged libel is contained in a newspaper or book published abroad the plaintiff can sue in this country even if the circulation is extremely limited.

Examples

In *Packard v Eleftherotypia* (1987), unreported, Commander Packard was awarded what were then record damages of £450,000 for a libellous article in a Greek magazine, of which only 87 copies were circulated in the UK.

This case should be contrasted with the case of *Pillai v Sarkar* (1994) *The Times*, 21 July. The alleged libel was contained in an English language periodical which had a circulation of 73,000 in India and 15 in England. One of the defendants sought to have a writ for damages which had been served on him for libel in England set aside. The judge held that England was not the natural forum for the issues in the case and that Calcutta was clearly and distinctly the more appropriate forum; this would apply even if the plaintiff confined his claim for damages to injury suffered in England. If followed, this case could significantly affect the number of actions where substantial damages are awarded in this country even though the circulation of the alleged libel here is extremely limited. (See also Section V, Chapter 11.)

In 1995 the European Court of Justice gave a ruling in *Shevill v Presse-Alliance SA* [1992] 1 All ER 409. In that case a Miss Fiona Shevill sued Presse Alliance, a French company, over an article in the newspaper *France-Soir*. The article stated that French police had made a drugs raid at a Bureau de Change operated by the company, Chequepoint, where Miss Shevill worked. She was referred to by name in the article and she sued for libel in England; 237,000 copies of *France-Soir* were sold in France, only 250 were sold in England and only five in York where the plaintiff lived. It was held that the plaintiff had an option to sue either in England or France but that she would be bound by the laws of libel in the country where she chose to sue. This decision was upheld by both the European Court of Justice and the Court of Appeal at the House of Lords in the UK (see Section V, Chapter 11).

An interesting case in 1993 involved the writer, Mr Graham Lord. He wrote a synopsis of a proposed biography of the thriller writer, Mr John le Carré and, as is customary, he sent it to his agent, who then sent it to nine publishers. John le Carré claimed that the synopsis was defamatory and threatened to sue for libel since there had been publication to a third party, albeit very limited.

Who to sue?

Consideration should be given to who can be sued. Where a writ for libel or slander is issued, it is necessary, as in all litigation, to identify the proposed defendant. In the case of slander normally only one individual will be made a defendant, but in the case of libel there may be a considerable number of defendants whom the plaintiff can elect to join or omit from the writ as he wishes. In the case, for example, of a newspaper, the newspaper proprietor, the editor and the journalist can all be sued. In some cases only the newspaper holding company will be sued and in rare cases, only the journalist will be sued. The usual practice is to join the editor, the journalist and the newspaper company. While there have been cases where a newsagent or distributor has been joined to proceedings (see *Goldsmith v Pressdram Ltd* [1977] 2 All ER 557 below), newsagents, wholesalers and booksellers will normally have a defence of innocent dissemination (see Section II, Chapter 7).

In the case of television, this could be the television company, the producers of the programme and any journalists featured in it. In the case of defamation in a book, the printer, publisher and author can all be sued. In practice, the printers are rarely joined and again it is unusual to find an author sued without the publisher. Printers will invariably have an indemnity from the publishers. A disclaimer denying any connection to any living person, which is frequently seen at the beginning of a novel, has no legal effect but it can count in mitigation.

Example

In 1995 Michael Foot sued the *Sunday Times* over claims that he had worked for the KGB during the Cold War. Mr Foot's solicitors took the unusual step of joining Rupert Murdoch, the newspaper's proprietor, to the proceedings. The basis of the claim was that Mr Rupert Murdoch was a hands-on proprietor who would have had to sanction publication of the allegation. The *Sunday Times* lawyer tried to have Mr Rupert Murdoch's name removed from the libel proceedings but was unsuccessful and the matter was very quickly settled thereafter on payment of 'substantial damages and costs', reported to amount to £250,000.

Distributors, booksellers and libraries should not be joined to the initial proceeding because, as will be clear in Section II, they have a separate defence of innocent dissemination. Once, however, libraries, booksellers, bookshops or distributors have been notified of the alleged libel, they can be sued in the same way as the publishers if they continue to offer for loan, sell or broadcast the offending item.

Examples

In Sir James Goldsmith's celebrated action against *Private Eye* in 1975 the distributors were notified of the alleged libel. *Private Eye* had published an item hinting that Sir James Goldsmith had been involved in assisting Lord Lucan to escape from the police after the latter's disappearance following the discovery of the murder of his children's nanny. Sir James Goldsmith issued writs for defamation against *Private Eye*, notified all the distributors of the alleged libel and subsequently issued 80 writs against the distributors who, after notification, could no longer avail themselves of the defence of innocent dissemination.

A similar situation occurred with the libel action brought by the Prime Minister, John Major, against the *New Statesman* over a denial of a rumour that he was involved with Downing Street cook, Miss Clare Latimer, who herself also sued for libel. In that case distributors such as W H Smith, after notification that that particular issue of the *New Statesman* contained an alleged libel, could not avail themselves of the defence of innocent dissemination and the Prime Minister and Miss Clare Latimer were widely believed to have recovered £60,000 damages in settlements from the printers and distributors. The eventual settlement with the magazine was for damages of £1,001. Of course in that case the printers and distributors, as is usual, had an indemnity from the magazine so that the actual costs the magazine had to meet were far greater than the damages it itself paid.

Obviously the defence of innocent dissemination cannot apply to a publication which is reasonably likely to contain defamatory material. It was for this reason that W H Smith the wholesale distributors and newsagent group refused for many years to distribute *Private Eye*. More recently a Mr and Mrs Anglesea sued printers and distributors of the satirical magazine *Scallywag* on the basis that the printers must have been aware of *Scallywag*'s reputation and therefore could not have been innocent disseminators. The case was settled on the basis of payment of damages and a statement in open court.

In 1995 a television journalist successfully sued the Department of Trade and Industry (DTI) for libel, naming Michael Heseltine, the then DTI President and ministers Richard Needman and Ian Taylor. He alleged they had signed letters sent out to members of the public which stated that Mr Gregory, the producer of the television programme *Dispatches* had produced a programme that was contrived and scaremongering (*Martyn Gregory v DTI* (1995), unreported). The programme was concerned with the export by British manufacturers of torture instruments. Martyn Gregory was awarded £40,000 damages together with costs. The case also showed some public concern as to whether the taxpayers or the ministers concerned should be responsible for the legal costs.

This case also shows the advantage that funding can be to a party to a libel action. The Police Federation will normally pay for police officers to bring libel proceedings and there has been a proliferation of such actions in recent years. On the other hand, when the former chairman of Cornwall Health Care Trust, Abigail Kirby-Harris, sued her fellow committee members for libel, and they sought to rely on a statutory defence, it was made clear that the National Health Service would not assist them in defending the proceedings (see Section II, Chapter 7).

Initial steps

Practical considerations

On a practical note it is of vital importance that matters should be dealt with in relation to defamation with the utmost speed. All details should be obtained from the client as to why he considers the passage defamatory. If the words are not defamatory on the face of them, then investigation needs to be made into the facts and matters which will support any innuendo which must be specified in the pleadings (see Section IV, Chapter 10.) The client must be clearly identified in the alleged defamatory material either by name, or by evidence from witnesses that from the information they had when they read the defamatory words, they understood them to refer to the plaintiff. If the defamation is of a group of persons, for example, police officers, then evidence must be given to show that the group is small and precisely defined enough for the plaintiff to be clearly identified within that group. Finally, evidence needs to be obtained as to publication and the extent of it.

In addition to acting quickly it is important that the client should be asked for his objectives. If it is a serious defamation the first objective may be to prevent further publication or to have an apology published or broadcast immediately with the question of damages being considered at a later date. A full letter before action must be prepared setting out precisely the details of the alleged libel and the remedies sought by the client. These matters will be examined in greater detail in Sections IV and V. The client must also be made aware of the financial implications of taking a libel action through to trial: there is no legal aid for libel and a successful plaintiff will only recover approximately two-thirds of his legal costs.

Cases of libel and slander are automatically tried by a jury (as the plaintiff is entitled to be judged by a jury of his peers) by virtue of s 69 of the Supreme Court Act 1991.

A party may apply for trial by a judge alone if the case is scientifically complex or otherwise cannot conveniently be tried by a jury. This arose in *Upjohn v BBC* (1994), unreported; the case concerned the nature of the drug Halcion (see Section II, Chapter 3). Similarly, in *McDonalds v Steel and Morris* [1995] 3 All ER 615 the so-called *McLibel* case which has been running since June 1994, there is no jury (see Section II, Chapter 3).

Check list

(1) Is the statement defamatory? Are the words defamatory or is there a defamatory innuendo? What are the facts?

(2) Is the plaintiff identifiable? Is he named or otherwise identified by reference to a location or organisation?

(3) If he is not named, is there evidence from people to whom the alleged libel has been published that they understood it to refer to him?

(4) Has there been publication to a third party? If so, how extensively?

(5) Is the plaintiff an individual or a company? Does the plaintiff have the right to sue?

(6) What are his objectives? Is the most important priority the publication of an apology, is it to obtain damages, or is it a combination of these factors?

(7) Is he prepared to take the matter through to trial with the enormous costs risk that this could involve, as there is no legal aid for libel?

(8) Who will be the defendants?

Section II

The Defendant

This Section examines the nominal and substantive defences. A brief examination in made of the nominal defences and then each of the substantive defences in the following five chapters. It is usually the practice in defamation actions to plead not only the appropriate nominal defences, but a number of other defences in the alternative.

Chapter 3—Justification

Definition
Application
Truth of the facts
Meaning
Preliminary ruling— RSC Ord 82, r 3A
Standard of proof
Evidence
Repetition
Reputation
Discovery
Rehabilitation of Offenders Act 1974
Practical considerations

Chapter 4—Fair Comment

Definition
Application
Test of fairness of comment
Truth of facts
Evidence
Public interest
Mixture of fact and comment

Death
General bad reputation
Jest—vulgar abuse
Public figure
Statutory defence
Apology
Payment into court
Security for costs

Nominal defences

Meaning of words

The first nominal defence is that the words of which complaint is made are not defamatory as alleged or defamatory of the plaintiff at all. The plaintiff in his statement of claim (Section IV, Chapter 10) will set out the defamatory meanings of which he complains. Since 1994 it is now open to a defendant at an early stage of the proceedings to apply to the court under Ord 82, r 3(A) of the Rules of the Supreme Court (RSC) for a ruling as to whether or not the words can bear the alleged meaning or whether they are capable of being defamatory at all.

Examples

A claim alleging defamation was made in respect of the book *Francis Bacon: His Life and Violent Times*. The claim, by a former neighbour of the late Francis Bacon, was made against the publishers and the author. The passage complained of related to Francis Bacon's great generosity to a young male companion and his family towards the end of his life. In an application to the court for a preliminary ruling on meaning, it was held that the particular words of the alleged defamatory material complained of (namely that Francis Bacon had been exploited by the family of his friend), were not capable of the defamatory meaning alleged.

In 1995, the actor and director Steven Berkoff sued a columnist, Julie Burchill, and the *The Times* newspaper over two articles in the *Sunday Times* (*Berkoff v Times Newspapers* (1996) *The Times*, 6 August). In the first, Miss Burchill wrote that: '... film directors from Hitchcock to Berkoff are notoriously hideous-looking people'. Nine months later, reviewing the film *Frankenstein*, she described the creature by saying, *inter alia*, '... it's a lot like Steven Berkoff only marginally better looking'. Mr Berkoff started proceedings for libel and claimed that the two articles meant that he was 'hideously ugly'. The newspaper sought a preliminary ruling that the words were not capable of being defamatory but it was held by the judge and upheld by the Court of Appeal that these words were capable of being defamatory of the plaintiff. The Court of Appeal held therefore that it was proper to leave the matter to the jury to decide whether the words were in fact defamatory. This is a significant decision which could have implications for satirical magazines and similar TV and radio programmes.

An application to the judge was made in the case of *Botham v Khan* (1996) *The Times*, 15 July for a preliminary ruling on meaning. The case arose out of a statement by the defendant, the cricketer Imran Khan, that 'all the leading bowlers in the last 20 years' had been guilty of illegal ball tampering. Mr Khan claimed that he did not consider ball tampering to be cheating although it was clear that what he had alleged was contrary to a rule of cricket. In the ruling on meaning the Court of Appeal in July 1996 held that what was important was what the plaintiff Ian Botham was said to have done, not whether or not Mr Khan thought that what he had done was cheating or not. The words were held capable of the defamatory meaning alleged although whether they were in fact defamatory was to be left to the jury. In fact despite the abandonment of the plea of justification, the jury found that the words were not defamatory. (See Section II, Chapter 3, below.)

Reference to plaintiff

The second nominal defence is that the words complained of have not been understood to refer to the plaintiff. The hurdles which a plaintiff has to overcome to establish this where he is not named, and where there is a class action, have already been examined (Section I, Chapter 2).

Example

In December 1995, two policemen, Wright and Callaghan, successfully sued the BBC over a *Panorama* programme, which they claimed had portrayed them as racist. The programme, which was entitled 'Race Hate UK', did not name the constables but they claimed that they were identifiable to colleagues and to the public in East London where they worked. The film showed them as racist officers, who for no reason other than his race and colour, arrested an Asian shopkeeper who was later acquitted of assaulting a white customer. The evidence given by the police officers established, to the jury's satisfaction, that the portrayal could be understood to refer to them and they both recovered damages. The alternative defence of fair comment failed (see Section II, Chapter 4).

Publication to third party

The third nominal defence is that there has been no publication to a third party. If the defendant can show that the communication was made only to the plaintiff, in circumstances where only the plaintiff would read the defamatory statement, then he can show that there has been no publication to a third person.

Substantive defences

The substantive defences for which the onus of proof is on the defendant are:

- Justification: this means proving that the words were true.
- Fair comment: this is a defence that the words complained of are fair comment made in good faith and without malice on a matter of public interest.
- Privilege: the plea is that the words were published on an occasion of absolute or qualified privilege.
- Unintentional defamation: a statutory defence under s 4 of the Defamation Act 1952, and retained in an amended form in ss 2–4 of the Defamation Act 1996.

In Chapter 7, further defences or matters which may assist a defendant are examined as follows:

- Consent:*Volenti non fit injuria*: the plaintiff consented to the libel.
- Accord and satisfaction: the plaintiff has already agreed to forego his right to sue and has been compensated.
- Mitigation.
- Statute of Limitation, Limitation Act 1980 as amended by s 5 of the Defamation Act 1996: time for issuing proceedings, namely after one year, has expired.
- Innocent dissemination: the defendant is a bookseller, library or distributor.
- Death: if either party to a libel or slander action dies, the action ceases.
- General bad reputation.
- Jest or vulgar abuse: the alleged libel would not be taken seriously.
- Public figure: the position of the plaintiff is that he must expect public criticism.
- Statutory defence: there is a defence of a statute law, s 1 of the Defamation Act 1996.

- Apology.
- Payment into court.
- Security for costs.

Chapter 3

Justification

Definition

Justification is the plea that the defamatory words are true. To sustain such a plea it is necessary to prove to the satisfaction of the jury, by admissible evidence, that the words were 'true in substance and in fact'. Proof of the defendant's belief in the truth of the words is not sufficient, nor is it sufficient to prove that a defamatory rumour existed: proof of the truth of the facts on which the rumour is based is required.

Example

In *Lewis v Daily Telegraph Ltd* [1964] AC 234 (see also Section I, Chapter 1), the *Daily Telegraph* published an article stating that the Fraud Squad was investigating the company. The newspaper was able to prove, as a statement of fact, that the Fraud Squad were investigating the company. However, the plaintiff succeeded and recovered damages because the newspaper was unable to prove the truth of the natural implication of the words, namely that there was fraud in the company to be investigated. The matter went to appeal and was subsequently settled out of court without a new trial.

As stated above, the falsity of the defamatory words is presumed in the plaintiff's favour (see Section I, Chapter 1).

Application

This defence applies to statements of fact, as distinct from comment or expressions of opinion. To succeed the defendant must prove the truth of the gist or sting of the libel.

Example

In *Dering v Uris* (1964) 2 QB 669 the plaintiff was a Polish doctor who had been a prisoner in the Auschwitz concentration camp. In his book

Exodus, Leon Uris had accused the plaintiff of cruelty in operations carried out in the camp, particularly in performing operations without anaesthetic. The defendant produced evidence that the plaintiff had conducted operations callously and the jury awarded a halfpenny damages.

There is also a provision under s 5 of the Defamation Act 1952 which states:

> *Justification*
> In an action for libel or slander in respect of words containing two or more distinct charges against the plaintiff, a defence of justification shall not fail by reason only that the truth of every charge is not proved if the words not proved to be true do not materially injure the plaintiff's reputation having regard to the truth of the remaining charges.

This means that if a defendant is not able to prove each particular allegation but can prove the gist of the allegation, the defence will not necessarily fail if each and every allegation cannot be proved to be true. So, for example, if the alleged libel is that the plaintiff had committed eight burglaries but the defendant was only able to prove six burglaries, the defence of justification could succeed. The essence of the defence of justification is that the plaintiff should not be entitled to recover damages for real or perceived damage to a reputation to which he is not entitled.

Examples

The proviso to s 5 was successfully invoked by the defendants in a Scottish case similar to *Dering v Uris* involving alleged war crimes. In *Gecas v Scottish Television* (1992), unreported, Anthony Gecas sued Scottish Television over a programme *Crimes of War* which claimed that he had murdered hundreds of thousands of Jews. Since the action was brought many years after the event, it was difficult for the television company to obtain precise evidence. Although the defendants were not able to prove each particular allegation, the judge (sitting alone as juries do not sit for libel actions in Scotland) found that the defendants had not established all the facts alleged, but in view of the facts that they had proved true, the plaintiff's reputation was not damaged by those that they could not prove. A contrast is provided by the case of *Wakeley v Cooke* (1849) 4 Ex Ch 511 where it was held that proof that once in his career a journalist was forced to apologise did not justify the statement that the reporter was a 'libellous journalist'. The words were held to imply a habitual tendency to be libellous.

Truth of facts

What is necessary to establish justification is proof that will stand up in open court of the truth of the words complained of. Witnesses should be supported by documentary or other evidence wherever possible.

Examples

Cordelia Lim, a nurse who worked for a cosmetic surgeon, was criticised in an article in the *News of the World* under the headline 'Agony of patient scarred forever'. The article alleged that Miss Lim left her patients seriously scarred after unsuccessful cosmetic surgery. She sued for libel and the newspaper pleaded justification. Witnesses gave evidence of their injuries, and photographs of their scars were produced. The jury accepted that the words were true and Miss Lim lost her case and subsequent appeal (*Lim v News of the World* (1990), unreported).

As indicated earlier, intent is irrelevant to a libel action (except in relation to malice and the Rehabilitation of Offenders Act 1974, see Section III, Chapter 3 below) so that if the defendant intended to defame the plaintiff and is nonetheless able to prove that the words are true, the plaintiff will not be entitled to damages.

As well as the burden of proof, an additional hazard for a defendant is that if he should plead justification but the plea fails, the plaintiff can be awarded aggravated damages on the grounds that the defendant had persisted in his allegations in open court, and in effect further publicised the libel. However, in the case brought by Ian Botham and Allan Lamb against the Pakistani cricketer, Imran Khan in 1996, Khan abandoned the plea of justification during the trial but the jury nonetheless found in favour of the defendant.

If, however, the defendant succeeds in proving the truth of part of the defence only, he is entitled to rely on that in mitigation in relation to any part of the plea not proved. In that event, the jury decides whether the words not proved to be true do injure the plaintiff's reputation, having regard to those proved to be true, as in *Gecas v Scottish Television* above.

In considering the alleged defamatory words, consideration must also be given to the context in which the words are set. This is of particular relevance in cases where the headline may be more defamatory than the article to which it refers. The defendant may succeed in establishing the truth of the facts in the article but may not be able to prove the headline. This particularly affects the press, since it is not unknown for a sub-editor to add a headline after the article itself has been passed by the newspaper's lawyers.

Example

In *Tudor Roberts v Private Eye* (1985), unreported, the plaintiff, an accountant, successfully sued *Private Eye* over an article alleging that the plaintiff had conspired to conceal a fraud over a charity golf tournament. While the article did not reveal fraud, the defendants were not able to justify the headline which referred to fraud, and the plaintiff recovered damages.

Meaning

It is an obvious principle that in deciding whether the words complained of are defamatory, the meaning of the words must first be decided.

Where the defamatory statement of fact has only one meaning, such as, for example, the plaintiff is a murderer, then the defendant's plea of justification will be to that natural and ordinary meaning only. Where, however, the words have a number of different meanings, or are defamatory by innuendo, the plaintiff will plead those meanings and may indeed plead all defamatory meanings the words can possibly sustain. The defendant is entitled in his defence to contend that the words had a less defamatory meaning than that relied on by the plaintiff and he can go on to plead to that less defamatory meaning. In doing so he may, of course, run the risk that should the judge find that the plaintiff's meanings are sustainable, the defence will not be directed to those less defamatory meanings. For example, if the plaintiff pleads that the defamatory passage means that he was dishonest and the defendant states that the meaning is only that the defendant was careless and seeks to prove that that is true, and if the jury find that the plaintiff's meaning of dishonesty is the one which the words bear, then the defendant will not have pleaded to that meaning and would not have a defence.

Example

An illustration of the complexity of meaning arose in *Tobias v Mail on Sunday* (1989), unreported. The newspaper ran an article under the headline 'Back Street Spaghetti Mountain' alleging that a trader was selling goods well beyond their sell-by-date. The plaintiffs claimed that the article meant that they knowingly sold food that was unsafe for human consumption. The paper contended that it simply meant that they sold secondhand food which could be unfit for human consumption. The paper produced three witnesses, all of whom confirmed that they had purchased food of a poor quality or past the sell-by-date and had not been stopped at the checkout. The newspaper, however, failed to prove the implication pleaded by the plaintiffs that the words meant they knowingly sold such food. It was held the words were capable of this meaning, and the plaintiffs recovered £470,000 damages.

Preliminary ruling—RSC Ord 82, r 3A

One of the recent reforms, which should have a material effect on libel actions, has been the amendment to RSC Ord 82 with effect from 1 September 1994. The new r 3A provides that any time after service of the statement of claim, either party can apply to a judge in chambers for a ruling as to whether the words complained of can bear the meanings alleged in the pleadings. If the judge decides that none of the words can bear the meanings alleged, the claim can be dismissed or judgment can be given or another appropriate order made. This is likely in the long term to have the effect of both limiting the costs of libel actions and encouraging early settlement.

Examples

In *Skuse v Granada Television* (1992) *The Independent*, 2 April Dr Frank Skuse, a Home Office forensic scientist, sued Granada Television over a *World in Action* programme which queried the soundness of the convictions of six Irishmen accused of an IRA bombing (the Birmingham Six). The programme stated that Dr Skuse had been wrong in his forensic tests. It was held on a preliminary ruling that this was capable of meaning that Dr Skuse was negligent as a forensic scientist and expert witness.

Such a preliminary ruling was also obtained in the cases of *Gillick v BBC* (1995) *The Times*, 20 October, *Charleston v News Group Newspapers* [1995] 2 AC 65 (see Section 1, Chapter 2), *Berkoff v Burchill* (1996) *The Times*, 9 August and *Botham v Khan* (1996) *The Times*, 15 July (see under 'Nominal defences' under Section II, p 37).

The second recent reform, also under Ord 82, r 3(2A) (hailed as a change which levels the playing field for defendants) provides that where the plea of justification, namely that the words are true, is relied on, then the plaintiff must specifically admit or deny any allegation claimed by the defendant to be true, and also specify the facts and matters upon which reliance is being placed in opposition to the defendant. The practical effect of this is that both parties will know the strength of the case against them at an earlier stage than previously.

Although these rule changes have been criticised, on the grounds that libel actions may have prolonged interlocutory proceedings with increased expense, the practical effect is likely to be that speculative actions could be deterred. The plaintiff will be unable to give fanciful meanings because of the risk that the defendant will have them struck out under Ord 82, r 3(A). This provision that the plaintiff must specifically admit or deny allegations claimed by the defendant to be true, will also make the defendant aware after service of the defence of the case he has to meet, and could result in prompt settlement negotiations.

Standard of proof

The test of what could be pleaded in the defence of justification used to be 'clear and sufficient evidence' before counsel to support the plea see, for example, *Associated Leisure v Associated Newspapers* [1970] 2 QB 450. However, in the case of *McDonalds v Morris and Steel* [1995] 3 All ER 615, CA the Court of Appeal laid down clear instructions as follows: a pleader must not put a plea on the record lightly and it is necessary that the defendant should:

(a)   believe the words complained of to be true;

(b)   intend to support the defence of justification at trial; and

(c)   have reasonable evidence to support the plea or reasonable grounds to suppose that sufficient evidence will be available at trial.

Where advice is called upon before publication, in relation to statements of facts which are clearly defamatory, it is advisable firstly, to ensure that before publication any contemporaneous reporters' notes or tapes should be retained and secondly, that signed statements should be obtained from witnesses. If such contemporaneous notes are not in existence, the jury may find it difficult to accept the defendant's plea of justification. This particularly applies to journalists, since juries, as has been seen, tend to favour the plaintiff and to disbelieve journalists, particularly where a tabloid newspaper is involved.

Where the defamatory statement is of a conviction for a criminal offence, then under s 12 of the Defamation Act 1996, proof of the conviction of the plaintiff is, in defamation actions, conclusive proof that the offence was committed. This provision does not extend to the plaintiff's witnesses or the defendant or his witnesses.

Examples

In *Connery v Sun* (1992), unreported, actor Jason Connery, sued the *Sun* over a statement that he was afraid to fight in the Gulf War. At the trial, the plaintiff denied making any such statements, and the journalist who alleged that she had tape recorded the comments was unable to produce the tapes; he recovered £35,000 damages.

In *Johnson v Radio City* (1988), unreported, a local radio station broadcast interviews from disappointed holidaymakers who had gone to a caravan site in the South of France and found that it was not up to the standard claimed in the brochure. The owner of the site sued in person, and evidence was given that the disc jockey, in preparing his scripts and interviews to be broadcast, had ignored statements from a number of satisfied holidaymakers who had no complaints about the site. The satisfied holidaymakers were called as witnesses by the plaintiff, and although almost an equivalent number of dissatisfied holidaymakers gave evidence on behalf of the defendant, the plea of justification failed and the owner of the caravan site was awarded £350,000 damages.

The difficulty and expense in succeeding in a plea of justification was also well illustrated in *Orme v Associated Newspapers Ltd* (1981) *The Times*, 4 February, where the Leader of the Unification Church (the Moonies) in Britain sued Associated Newspapers over an article in the *Daily Mail*. This had claimed that the Moonies was a sinister organisation which brainwashed young people and broke up families. The case lasted 100 days and over 117 witnesses were called. The jury found that the article was true and the plaintiff was ordered to pay costs, estimated at nearly £500,000.

A similar plea of justification in a high profile case of similar length and number of witnesses arose in *Lord Aldington v Tolstoy and Watts* (1989), unreported. The alleged libel, circulated in 10,000 pamphlets, was that Lord Aldington at the end of the Second World War had been involved in repatriation of prisoners of war to Russia, where their fate was certain death. The defendant author, Nikolai Tolstoy, had obtained a considerable amount of evidence while researching a book on this subject, but despite the many witnesses, including surviving ex-prisoners, flown in from Eastern Europe the jury found that the statement was not proved to be true and awarded Lord Aldington record libel damages of £1.5m.

This case illustrates another pitfall of libel, since some seven years after the case was heard, the plaintiff has received neither costs nor damages. Also Tolstoy has successfully appealed to the European Court of Human Rights which held the original award was an infringement of his right to freedom of expression under art 10 of the European Convention on Human Rights. (See Section V, Chapter 11.)

Evidence

As can be seen from the above cases, evidence of truth can be both difficult to obtain, expensive and even then not accepted by the jury. In all cases of justification, full particulars must be given of the facts and matters relied on to support the plea. As stated above, the purpose of a libel action is to obtain recompense for damage to reputation, that is, the reputation which the plaintiff has at the time of the trial. If therefore, at the time of publication, the defendant is not in a position to prove the truth of the defamatory statements, for example that the plaintiff is dishonest, but shortly after publication, the plaintiff is convicted of theft, the defendant is entitled to rely on that fact in pleading justification. It is important that a fact so relied, on if post-publication, must be close to the date of publication, since the general rule is that acts and conduct on the part of the plaintiff occuring after the date of publication are not usually admitted.

Examples

In *Judge v Guardian Newspapers Ltd* (1995), unreported, the plaintiff, Paul Judge, was the Director-General of the Conservative Central Office. The *Guardian* had published an article alleging that he had delayed in co-operating with the request by Asil Nadir's (of the company Polly Peck) trustee in bankruptcy for details of payments made by his companies to the Conservative Party. The article was published on 15 September 1993. In their particulars of justification, the defendants relied, *inter alia*, upon the fact that a proper reply to a repeated query was not received until 21 October 1993. Judge lost his action in January 1995, and later dropped his appeal.

In *Godman v The Times* [1926] 2 KB 273 it was held that evidence relating to incidents similar to the libel could be adduced. In this case, the plaintiff sued over a statement that he had been involved in a conspiracy to defraud shipowners by pretending a cargo had been seized by pirates. The defendants pleaded justification and referred to two other incidents involving the plaintiff where cargoes had been transferred or scuttled and false insurance claims made. It was held by the Court of Appeal, on the plaintiff's application to strike out the particulars relating to the other two ships, that they were entitled to remain as part of the defence.

In *Jackson v Mirror Group Newspapers Ltd* (1994) *The Times*, 29 March an interesting point arose concerning the defendant's entitlement to evidence. In that case, the well-known singer, Michael Jackson, had sued the *Daily Mirror* for libel over photographs of him and articles which they had published in four issues of the paper, which he claimed meant that he had become 'hideously distorted and disfigured by plastic surgery'. It was held by the Court of Appeal that a defendant to a defamation action, where allegations concerning the appearance of the plaintiff were involved, was entitled to a stay of the action unless and until the plaintiff submitted to a medical examination on behalf of the defendant. It was also held that the defendant's medical expert was entitled to discovery of relevant medical records under the care and control of the plaintiff's doctor.

Another example of the successful use of defence of justification was the action brought by two police officers against the *People* newspaper (*Williams and Baker v The People* (1991), unreported). The *People* called witnesses who said that the two officers had remained in a panda car and had done nothing to help three fellow officers who were being beaten up during a New Year's Day riot in Devon. The plea of justification was upheld and the two officers were ordered to pay the costs of the hearing. By contrast, the defence of justification failed in the case where the former head of the Obscene Publications Squad, Mr Bennett, in 1995 sued *For Women* magazine. He claimed he was portrayed in the article as a sick and evil transvestite and a storming hypocrite. Although evidence was given that Mr Bennett had dressed up in women's clothes for family parties and did a Benny Hill impersonation, he succeeded in recovering £15,000 damages.

In *Upjohn v BBC* (1994), unreported, the American manufacturer of the sleeping drug, Halcion, sued the BBC over a *Panorama* programme entitled 'The Halcion Nightmare', which claimed that the company and its physician had misled the regulatory authorities about the side effects of the drug. The programme was broadcast after the drug was banned in the UK and included interviews with patients who had taken the pill and two representatives from Upjohn. The case lasted for nearly six months, involved a considerable amount of expert evidence and was (unusually for a libel action), heard before a judge alone because of its technical complexity. The defence was of justification, but the judge held that, although Upjohn had made serious errors when it informed regulators about tests on Halcion, it had not done so intentionally or dishonestly. He awarded the company £60,000 damages. However the Professor of Psychiatry who appeared as an expert witness in the programme and counterclaimed against Upjohn, was awarded £50,000 damages, because the judge held that Upjohn had made defamatory comments in their criticisms of him.

In the longest running libel action in the world, which started in June 1994, the international high street restaurant chain, McDonalds, is suing two defendants, David Morris and Helen Steel, for libel. McDonalds allege that the defendants distributed leaflets outside its UK headquarters and certain restaurants, which contained numerous defamatory statements and serious allegations. The leaflet was produced by Green Peace, the international environmental pressure group, in London and claimed that:
(a)   food from McDonalds was unhealthy;
(b)   the food caused an increased risk of cancer;
(c)   the corporation had contributed to global environmental problems, such as destruction of the rain forests to create pastures for cattle and the puncturing of the ozone layer;
(d)   McDonalds was hostile to trade unions;
(e)   McDonalds was an exploitative employer;

(f)   its meat was prepared in such a way as to be cruel to animals;
(g)   the company's advertising deliberately ensnared children.

The two defendants, who are unemployed and representing themselves (there is no legal aid for libel), are pleading the defences of justification and fair comment.

While the pleading is not evidence it must set out the case the plaintiff has to meet. Hearsay or the defendant's belief or evidence that there was a rumour to that effect concerning the plaintiff will not be sufficient, except to the limited extent outlined in *Aspro Travel Ltd v Owners Abroad Group plc* (1996) 1 WLR 132 (see Section I, Chapter 1).

As in all litigation but particularly in libel, where there is a conflict of evidence, the jury may accept the version of the plaintiff. A jury may find it hard to believe that a plaintiff would put himself through the strain and expense of a public trial unless he felt compelled to do so. There have been a number of cases where, even when two or three journalists gave evidence contrary to the plaintiff's, the jury have still believed the plaintiff (*Lord Linley v Today* (1990), unreported (Section III, Chapter 9), *Moore v News of the World* (1971) *The Times*, 12 May (Section II, Chapter 7)).

Examples

In a celebrated action by the politician and author Lord Archer *(Jeffrey Archer v Daily Star* (1987), unreported), Mr Archer as he then was, sued the *Star* newspaper over a claim that he had had sexual relations with a prostitute. It was not disputed that he arranged for £2,000 to be paid to the prostitute to go abroad but, although the prostitute gave evidence that she had had sexual relations with the plaintiff, the jury did not believe her, preferring the evidence of Lord Archer and Mary Archer, whom the judge referred to as his 'fragrant' wife. Lord Archer was awarded £500,000 damages and the judge specifically recommended to the jury that the fact that the newspaper had persisted in its allegations to the bitter end should be reflected in the award. Again, no journalists' notes were in existence.

In the case brought by a food retailer, Tobias, against the *Mail on Sunday* over an *exposé* of food being sold after the sell-by-date (see under 'Meaning' above), the writ was issued in 1984, but the case did not come for trial until 1989, by which time some of the evidence had been disposed of and journalists' notes also apparently destroyed.

The proposals by Lord Woolf to speed up civil proceedings and the alteration of the limitation period for libel actions from three years to one year (see Section V, Chapter 11) are likely to make such delays rarer.

Repetition

Where a party seeks to rely on affidavit evidence in other proceedings, it was held by the Court of Appeal in 1996 that this will not be sufficient to sustain a defence of justification. This is a significant ruling which could severely limit certain types of investigative journalism, since frequently, a newspaper may come into possession of affidavit evidence or pleadings, for example, in relation to proceedings in another country which they will not now be able to publish without proof of the truth of facts in any such affidavit.

Example

In the case of *Stern v Piper* (1996) *The Times,* 30 May, CA, the *Mail on Sunday* had published an article about the plaintiff, Stern, who had been declared bankrupt in 1978 and discharged in 1985. The article, under a headline referring to a £3m debt, claimed that the plaintiff had 'allegedly failed to honour debts of more than £3m'. The article gave details of a pending High Court action against the plaintiff and the companies with which he was associated, and relied on and quoted from an affirmation sworn by the senior partner of a firm of solicitors suing the plaintiff. The newspaper pleaded justification, and sought to allege that the words were substantially true, because they meant the plaintiff was once again in financial trouble and he was involved in High Court proceedings in which he was accused of the matters contained in the affirmation.

At first instance, the judge had refused to strike out the justification defence but the Court of Appeal took the view that while the defence of privilege (see Chapter 5) applied to a document read out in open court, that could not extend to documents not produced in open court. It was held that as in the present case only one side was reported, the affirmation could not form the basis for a defence of justification. The judgment examined to what extent privilege could be appropriate, but the key to the case and what was objected to, was the use of extracts from the affirmation in the defendant's particulars of justification. The core of the plaintiff's case was the so-called repetition rule that it is not a defence to an action for libel for the defendant to prove that he was merely repeating what he had been told.

Reputation

It is open to the defendant to claim that even if the words were not true, the plaintiff's reputation has not been damaged by the alleged libel.

Examples

In 1976, the American actor Telly Savalas, then at the height of his Kojak fame, sued Associated Newspapers over a statement that his wild night-life while filming on location in Germany had led to him forgetting his lines and other delays on the set. The defence attempted to prove the truth of the statement, but also contended that he was still an interna-tional star and had not had his reputation harmed by the publication. This plea was not accepted, and he recovered £34,000 damages.

In another celebrated case in 1978, Vanessa Redgrave and other mem-bers of her Workers Revolutionary Party sued the *Observer* over an arti-cle which alleged that the Party was brainwashing its members and had an arms cache at its headquarters. Justification was pleaded but the plea failed, because although the jury found that the words were not true, they did not award any damages because they held that the untrue words did not materially injure the reputation of the plaintiffs (see also Section I, Chapter 2); in other words, the plaintiffs were known as people of extreme views who might be expected to behave in the manner indi-cated.

In November 1996 Albert Reynolds, the former Irish Prime Minister, sued the *Sunday Times* over an allegation that he had lied to the Dail, the Irish Parliament. The newspaper pleaded justification and qualified privi-lege in a case which lasted six weeks. The jury found for Albert Reynolds but awarded no damages. He had rejected a payment into court of £5,005 but the judge later ruled that he should be awarded 1p.

An interesting case arose on reputation in *McNab v Associated News-papers* (1996) *The Times*, 17 May, CA. In that case, the plaintiff was a former member of the SAS who wrote books under the pseudonym, Andy McNab. He brought an action for libel against the *Daily Mail* over an article headed 'Andy McNab is a SAS hero but does he have a dark side?' The defendants sought an order that the plaintiff should state his true name on the writ and identify readers of the newspaper who knew his true name. The plaintiff lodged his true name in a sealed envelope in the court but the judge refused to order that the plaintiff should identify readers of the newspaper who knew his true name. In the Court of Ap-peal, the question was ventilated as to whether the plaintiff had a reputa-tion as 'Andy McNab' and whether his reputation in relation to his real name had been damaged over an article concerning 'Andy McNab'. These issues were left to the trial judge but it was ordered that the plaintiff should give particulars of persons who knew of his real identity.

Discovery

There will frequently be occasions where the defendant will not be in possession of sufficient evidence or documentation to provide full particulars of his plea of justification, but where the plaintiff himself is in possession of those documents. It is however established that the defendant may not defer filing the particulars of justification until after the discovery and no 'fishing expeditions' are normally allowed. A fishing expedition is where the defendant does not have the evidence required, but hopes that sufficient material will be disclosed by the plaintiff on discovery to enable him to sustain a defence. However, in a significant decision in *McDonalds v Steel and Morris* [1995] 3 All ER 615, CA, where the defendants had insufficient evidence but believed that the documentation required to support the plea would be disclosable by the plaintiffs on discovery or would be obtained by *subpoena* or during cross-examination, the Court of Appeal refused to strike out the defence. The court also took the opportunity to make important rulings on justification evidence and discovery.

Example

In this case McDonalds, the hamburger restaurant chain, in 1994, sued two members of an environmental pressure group over a pamphlet distributed outside their restaurant entitled *What's wrong with McDonalds?* (See 'Evidence' above). The pamphlet contained serious allegations against McDonalds, including the allegation that they had destroyed vast areas of rain forests to create pastures for cattle. The defence was of justification and fair comment and after a number of interlocutory proceedings, the plaintiffs applied to strike out the defence of justification and the particulars of justification. The application was successful at first instance and the defendants appealed. The Court of Appeal's ruling took the opportunity to make a thorough and detailed examination of the various stages at which evidence to support a defence of justification should be available.

Their Lordships dealt with the matter on the basis of the various stages of a libel action, and the procedure and recommendations which it laid down will be applicable to future actions. In summary, the points made were as follows:

(1) *Service of defence*: at this stage, the defendants should believe the words to be true, should intend to support the defence, and should have reasonable grounds to support the plea or reasonable grounds to suppose that sufficient evidence to prove the allegation would be available at trial.

(2) *Interlocutory application to strike out*: at this stage, after the exchange of witness statements, it might be apparent that the defence was unsupported.

(3)   *Onset of the trial*: at this stage, a further application could be considered to strike out to limit costs.

(4)   *Close of evidence*: at this stage all the evidence would be before the court and unsupported matters could be removed from the pleadings.

In the case before them, the court heard that while there were parts of the defendants' case which were weak, evidence might be forthcoming by the time of trial. The court was also entitled to take into account that the evidence on which a defendant may be entitled to rely at trial, may take a number of different forms:

(a)   his own evidence and the evidence of witnesses called on his behalf;

(b)   evidence obtained in Civil Evidence Act statements;

(c)   evidence contained in his own documents or documents produced by third parties on *subpoena*;

(d)   evidence elicited from the plaintiff or the plaintiff's witnesses in the course of cross-examination;

(e)   answers to interrogatories;

(f)   evidence contained in documents disclosed by the plaintiff on discovery.

This is a significant ruling which is likely to assist in those cases where part of the evidence required by the defendant may be in the possession of the plaintiff, but these precise guidelines will still prevent an unsupported defence and 'fishing expeditions' by the defendant.

Reference was made at this appeal to the new rule under RSC Ord 38 which came into effect in 1986 requiring the exchange of witness statements, from which it would be apparent what evidence there was to support the defence pleaded. However, it was pointed out that witness statements should not give rise to further interlocutory hurdles which the defendants' case would have to jump in order to be allowed to proceed to trial. The Court of Appeal held, instead of the 'clear and sufficient evidence' test previously applied, that the defendants should have reasonable evidence to support the plea of justification, 'or reasonable grounds for supposing that sufficient evidence to prove the allegations will be available at trial'. This would seem to allow the defendants to proceed even if all the evidence to support their particulars is not readily available.

Examples

In the libel action brought by the Tory MP, Neil Hamilton, and the lobbyist, Ian Greer, against the *Guardian* newspaper over the cash for questions controversy in 1996, the MP had lobbied successfully to have included in s 13 of the Defamation Act 1996 the provision which would allow an individual MP to waive parliamentary privilege for the purpose of pursuing a libel action (see Section V, Chapter 11). Having waived his privilege, the two plaintiffs, who were represented by the same counsel and solicitors, pursued the action with determination and vigour. However, as a result of matters disclosed in discovery the case was abandoned only the day before the trial. The *Guardian* had sought to *subpoena* both the Prime Minister and the Deputy Prime Minister together with a *subpoena duces tecum* (a subpoena directed to the production of documents) for documents to be disclosed by them. As a result of this discovery, it became apparent only days before the trial was due to start that there was a conflict of interest between the two plaintiffs. The action was settled the day before the trial on terms which included payment by each of the plaintiffs to the *Guardian* of £7,500 towards the newspaper's costs informally estimated at over £300,000.

In *Allen v Channel Four Television* (1992), unreported, an interesting case involving a successful plea of justification and showing the importance of discovery arose when the South African journalist and socialite Jani Allen sued Channel Four Television for libel. Jani Allen alleged that the portrayal of her in a documentary as the lover of the extreme right-wing leader in South Africa, Eugene Terre-Blanche, was untrue and defamatory. She denied in the witness box that she had had affairs or any kind of sexual relationship with Mr Terre-Blanche. A former flatmate of Jani Allen gave evidence that she had spied through a keyhole Mr Terre-Blanche's bottom rising and falling over the form of Miss Allen. In addition, half-way through the trial, the plaintiff's diary was delivered anonymously to the defendant's counsel. It contained detailed sexual fantasies, on which she was extensively cross-examined. The plea of justification was accepted by the jury, and Miss Allen was left to pick up a substantial bill for costs. While the evidence was a direct conflict, as was to be expected, the diary which had not been available to the defendant before trial and therefore was not disclosed on discovery, appeared to take the plaintiff by surprise. Normally exchange of witness statements and discovery will avoid this type of ambush.

A similar item produced in court, to the surprise of the plaintiff, brought about the successful plea of justification in *Taylforth v The Sun* (1994), unreported, brought by *Eastenders'* actress Gillian Taylforth against the *Sun* newspaper. The newspaper, allegedly tipped off by the police, had published an allegation that she had indulged in oral sex with her fiancé in a parked Range Rover on a sliproad off the A1. The allegation was vigorously denied by the plaintiff and her fiancé. The newspaper pleaded justification, and the policeman gave clear evidence of what he had seen.

The jury may well have been persuaded, however, by the production of a video, showing the plaintiff some years earlier at a party simulating oral sex with a sausage. The jury found that the plea of justification was upheld, and Miss Taylforth was left to pick up a bill for costs estimated at £500,000.

Rehabilitation of Offenders Act 1974

The provisions of this Act constitute a limited exception to the rule that proof of the truth of the words complained of will be a complete defence. The Act provides that, in relation to certain serious offences where the sentence of imprisonment is 30 months or less, a conviction shall be treated as spent for the purposes of the Act after a period of time specified, depending on the nature and extent of the sentence imposed. This gives a chance for a reformed prisoner to have the slate wiped clean. In the event of any proceedings over an allegation that the plaintiff had a conviction, where that conviction was at the time of publication a spent conviction, then if the plaintiff can prove that the defendant was actuated by malice in referring to the spent conviction notwithstanding that it is true, he can recover damages for libel. This is therefore an exception to the general rule that intent is irrelevant.

Practical considerations

As has been illustrated, the defence of justification is difficult, complex, expensive and can be counter-productive because of the risk of aggravated damages being awarded if the plea fails (see Section III, Chapter 9). The occasional successes illustrated above are rare, and in the vast majority of cases where the defence of justification is pleaded, it will either fail in open court or, because it cannot be sustained with sufficient particularisation or evidence, will lead to the settlement of the proceedings. It is therefore essential, despite some of the comments in *McDonalds v Steel and Morris* above, for those concerned with the publication or broadcast of statements of fact which may be defamatory, that the evidence, be it in documentary form or statements of evidence, is available before publication. If not, the necessary amendments to limit the published statements to what can be proved to be true should be made before publication.

If there is any doubt about the availability of evidence to support a plea of justification, a payment into court should be considered (see Chapter 7). Also a defendant should be warned that if he pleads justification and it fails, aggravated damages can be awarded on the grounds that he has persisted with his plea in open court (see Section III, Chapter

9). As has been seen, there is no legal aid for libel and consideration should also be given to the relevant financial standing of the plaintiff and the defendant.

It was anticipated that the new Defamation Act 1996 would contain a provision enabling a defendant in mitigation of damages to give evidence of specific facts or incidents of misconduct relating to the plaintiff's reputation in relation to the sector of his life to which the defamatory statement related; the current rule being that evidence of general bad reputation is admissible, but specific acts of misconduct are not. This would have prevented court abuses by the late Robert Maxwell, who was able to bring specific libel proceedings in circumstances where evidence of his reputation in business dealings could not be laid before the court. Unfortunately, the House of Commons voted against this proposal, the so-called 'muck-rakers charter' and the Defamation Act 1996 makes no change to the existing rule.

Check list

(1) What are the facts on which your client seeks to plead justification?

(2) What is the evidence of those facts?

(3) Are there, or can there be signed witness statements, together with documentary proof?

(4) Will there be sufficient evidence to provide effective particulars of justification or could there be a successful strike out application by the plaintiff?

(5) Can all the witnesses be found and will they sign statements?

(6) These witness statements should be taken as quickly as possible, since if particulars of justification cannot be sufficiently detailed to stand up to cross-examination, it could be appropriate for the defendant to apologise and/or consider a payment into court.

(7) The amount of a payment into court needs to be carefully considered. It should be sufficient to tempt the plaintiff, who must be prepared to make a discount for settlement, yet at the same time it should not be too high to enable the plaintiff to take a sum of money out which he would be unlikely to be awarded.

(8) The client should be fully aware that aggravated damages, even if not sought, can be awarded where a plea of justification is persisted with in open court but fails. If there is likely to be difficulty in obtaining sufficient evidence, it could be appropriate to have as strong a defence as possible and then open immediately without prejudice negotiations.

(9) Even if there was insufficient evidence at the time of publication, has the plaintiff done anything since publication which would affect or justify the defamatory statement made about him?

(10) The relative financial standing of the plaintiff and defendant should also be considered; is the plaintiff a private individual of limited means? Is the plaintiff being funded by his professional body or trade union? Is the defendant either a trade union, organisation or a substantial corporate body such as a newspaper?

Chapter 4

Fair Comment

Definition

Fair comment is the plea that the alleged defamatory words were fair comment or expressions of opinion as opposed to statements of fact, made without malice, on a matter of public interest. The defence is applicable to defamatory expressions of opinion. The basis of the defence is that an individual is entitled to express his own opinion provided it is honestly made, and that in making the statement he is not actuated by malice in the sense of spite, ill-will or improper motive. The facts on which the comment was made must be proved to be true at the time the comment was made. While the facts on which the comment was made must be proved to be true, the comment itself does not have to be true, but it has to be fair. Despite its superficial attractiveness, this defence, like justification, rarely succeeds in practice.

Application

For the defence of fair comment to succeed, the defendant has to prove that:

(a) the facts on which the comment is based are true and were true at the time the comment was made and were contained in or referred to in the publication complained of;

(b) the comment in light of the proved facts was one which a fair-minded person could make (even one with a strong or obstinate view);

(c) the comment was the honest expression of the opinion of the defendant made without malice;

(d) the comment did not go beyond being fair into the realm of invective or abuse.

Test of fairness of comment

For a defence of fair comment to succeed, it is essential that the comment or expression of opinion constitutes the defendant's honest belief.

Example

The most well-known test is that laid down in the case of *Merivale v Carson* (1887) 20 QBD 275 which is:

> Would any fair man, however prejudiced he may be, however exaggerated or obstinate his views, have come to this opinion based on these facts?

This was expanded in the case of *Silkin v Beaverbrook Newspapers Ltd* [1958] 2 All ER 516. In that case, the *Sunday Express* published an article critical of the plaintiff. It said on the one hand that the plaintiff in the House of Lords had spoken against combining forces with the Germans because of their war record. On the other hand, it said that he was chairman of Noble Motors who marketed a popular German car, Heinkels, in Britain. The judge put it to the jury 'could a fair-minded man, holding a strong view, holding perhaps an obstinate view, holding perhaps a prejudiced view—could a fair-minded man have been capable of writing this?'. It was held that the facts on which the comment was based were true and the jury found that the article was fair comment and the plaintiff lost his action.

Truth of facts

The facts on which the comment is based must be true and proved by the defendant to be true at the time the comment is made. If the defendant is not able to prove the truth of all the facts, the defence of fair comment can still succeed if the comment can be shown to be fair in relation to the facts which can be proved to be true. There is a similar provision under s 6 of the Defamation Act 1952, unchanged by the Defamation Act 1996, as applies to justification, covering the situation where not all the facts are proved to be true. Section 6 provides:

> *Fair Comment*
> In an action for libel or slander in respect of words consisting partly of allegations of fact and partly of expressions of opinion, a defence of fair comment shall not fail by reason only that the truth of every allegation of fact is not proved if the expression of opinion is fair comment having regard to such of the facts alleged or referred to in the words complained of as are proved.

The test to be applied is both objective and subjective. On the one hand the jury must be satisfied that, having regard to the facts proved to be true, the comment is one which an honest person can hold, viewed objectively. From a subjective point of view they have to be satisfied that, in this particular case, the comment was the honest belief of the defendant making the statement.

Evidence

First hand evidence should be given by the defendant to show his honest belief in the comments made, as well as the truth of the factual basis.

Examples

The plea of fair comment by the defendant newspaper succeeded in the case, *Meacher v Observer* (1988), unreported, involving the MP Michael Meacher who sued the *Observer* newspaper over an article stating that he had played down his middle-class origins for political advantage in the Labour Party. Another Labour MP, Brian Sedgemore sued *The Times* and its columnist Roy Kilroy-Silk (*Sedgemore v Times and Kilroy-Silk* (1990), unreported) over an article which claimed that the MP was exploiting the *Satanic Verses*/Salman Rushdie affair for the benefit of his standing in his constituency. The defence of fair comment was pleaded but the jury failed to agree and the case was abandoned. The case between two newspaper editors, likened by the judge to two colliding steam engines, showed again the difficulties of a successful plea of fair comment. In that case, *Neil and Sunday Times v Worsthorne* (1990), unreported, Andrew Neil, then editor of the *Sunday Times*, sued Peregrine Worsthorne, columnist on the *Sunday Telegraph*, over an article which made reference to Andrew Neil's relationship with a Miss Pamella Bordes, which Andrew Neil claimed implied he knew she was a prostitute at the time of his relationship with her. The defence of fair comment did not succeed and Andrew Neil was awarded £1,000 damages, the Sunday Times 60p.

Public interest

Whether or not a subject can be fairly said to be a matter of common interest has been judicially defined as a matter which is expressly or impliedly submitted to public criticism or contempt. The onus of proof is on the defendant to show that this is a matter of public interest. While it has been held that the private life of an author or artist is not a matter of public interest, there is no doubt that in these times of increasing publicity, which is seen as essential to the career of public performers and actively sought by them, that such persons may be said now to invite comment. In a similar way, a person who writes a letter to a newspaper which is published, thereby lays himself open to criticism in the same way as a public figure.

It is well established that it is a matter of public interest to comment on a public figure in relation to the way he conducts his public business. Under this category would come public criticism of ministers, MPs or local councillors about the way in which they conduct the business for which they were elected. Comment on their private lives in this country can be a matter of public interest if it is in relation to their ability to conduct that business. A statement, for example, that a person was no good at public meetings could be fair comment, and the plaintiff's conduct at public meetings could be relevant. However, a comment that the plaintiff was a poor gardener could not be a matter of public interest. Generally it is relatively straightforward for a defendant to establish the public interest element of the defence since it is defined fairly widely.

Examples

In *Wright and Callaghan v The BBC* (1996), unreported (see Section II, Chapter 3), two police officers sued the BBC over a *Panorama* programme which implied that they were racist in their arrest of an Asian shopkeeper later acquitted of assaulting a white man. The defence of fair comment failed but public interest was not disputed.

The MP, Peter Bottomley, sued the *Sunday Express* in 1995 over a story which accused him of betraying the Northern Ireland peace process by appearing on the same platform as a Sinn Fein leader. The article was entitled 'The Final Betrayal'. Evidence was given that he had given an interview with two journalists making it clear that he was attending the meeting on behalf of his peace group, New Dialogue, but none of this appeared in the article. The defence of fair comment failed. It was not disputed that the matter was of great public interest.

Fair comment obviously applies to reviews of plays, films, books etc but only in relation to the performances, since extraneous comment will go beyond the terms of the defence.

Example

In *Cornwell v News of the World* (1970), unreported, an article reviewing a play starring Charlotte Cornwell, the actress,   described her as 'wally of the week'. The reviewer stated 'She can't sing, her bum is too big, and she has the sort of stage presence that jams lavatories'. It was held that the words went beyond what could be fair comment. She was awarded £11,000 against which the newspaper appealed. Following a retrial, she was awarded £10,000.

The definitive statement on what constitutes fair comment, arose in *London Artists Ltd v Littler* [1969] 2 QB 375 when Lord Denning stated 'whenever a matter is such as to affect people at large, so that they may be legitimately interested in or concerned at what is going on, ... or what may happen to them or others; then it is a matter of public interest on which everyone is entitled to make fair comment'. In that case, the four stars of a successful West End play gave notice simultaneously, and a defamatory comment alleging a conspiracy to force the play off was made at a press conference by the producer. Although the judge at first instance held that the four leading members of the play simultaneously resigning could not be a matter of public interest, the decision was reversed on appeal where it was held that this was a matter of public interest. The plaintiffs were successful because the defendants were unable to prove the defamatory statement of fact that there had been a conspiracy.

In the case where the pharmaceutical company, Upjohn, sued the BBC in 1994, there was an attempt to plead fair comment as well as justification, but as has been seen the plea failed (see Chapter 3). The performance of a drug, however, was clearly a legitimate matter of public interest.

Mixture of fact and comment

For the comment to be fair, the facts on which it is based must be true. If the comment is based on a privileged report, then even if the facts contained in the privileged report are untrue, the comment can still be fair. Therefore fair comment is available as a defence only in relation to facts which are either true or, if untrue, were published on a privileged occasion. It can, therefore, follow that an honest opinion on true facts, if it is the genuine belief of the defendant, can be successfully defended by the plea of fair comment, even though the comment is untrue.

Examples

In *McCarthy and Stone v Daily Telegraph* (1993), unreported, the plaintiffs were builders marketing sheltered housing for the elderly. The *Daily Telegraph* had published an article critical of the financial details in the plaintiffs' advertising. The article alleged that in a number of cases, elderly people had been misled by the advertising and had ended up in a seriously disadvantaged financial position. In the action for libel, the defendants pleaded that the words were fair comment on a matter of public interest. The question of sheltered housing for the elderly, and particularly whether or not the financial inducements were misleading, was held to be a matter of public interest. The defendants provided evidence as to the truth of the factual basis for the comments and the case was abandoned half way through the trial by the plaintiffs.

The case of *Walker and Wingsail v Yachting World* (1994), unreported, involved a controversial yacht whose performance was reviewed critically in *Yachting World*. The facts were that certain claims were made by the plaintiffs, the manufacturer and design company, of the yacht's performance, but when it was tested independently with a *Yachting World* reporter on board, the performance was not nearly as impressive as had been claimed by the manufacturer. *Yachting World* said that the facts in its report were true. The magazine claimed that its article meant that the firm had made misleading claims recklessly; the plaintiffs claimed that the article meant they had made inflated claims of the yacht dishonestly, with the intention of misleading prospective purchasers. The issue was clearly a matter of public interest, but it was held that the words were capable of meaning that the yacht designer had acted dishonestly and deliberately. The defendants were not able to prove this and the plaintiffs were awarded the very substantial sum of £1,485,000, of which £1m was an award to the boat builder, a corporate plaintiff (Section I, Chapter 2), even though there was no claim for special damages (Section IV, Chapter 9). *Yachting World* appealed and the matter was subsequently settled shortly before the appeal on the basis of agreed damages of £160,000.

The difficulty of establishing which is fact and which is comment was clearly illustrated in the following case, which not only went to the House of Lords, but also to a retrial. In practice it is always safer to rely on justification as a defence as well as fair comment if at all possible, since if the words complained of are held to be statements of fact rather than comment then the defence of fair comment will fail as it will not be applicable.

Example

The case of *Vladimir Telnikoff v Vladimir Matusevich* [1992] 2 AC 343 arose out of an article which appeared in the *Daily Telegraph* by Vladimir Telnikoff, a Russian emigrant. He criticised the BBC Russian Service for being staffed with 'Russian speaking national minorities of the Soviet Union' with only 10 per cent associated with the Russian people. His article drew a letter in response (which was published) in the *Daily Telegraph* from Vladimir Matusevich, a Russian Jew, who claimed that Mr Telnikoff's article meant that people wishing to work in the BBC Russian Service should be subjected to a blood test. He went on to claim in the letter that Mr Telnikoff was advocating the dismissal of ethnically alien people. Mr Telnikoff sued for libel. Mr Matusevich claimed that his words were fair comment on what Mr Telnikoff had said, and that the references to blood testing, dismissals and ethnically alien people were inferences that could be drawn from Telnikoff's article. He also sought to have the article which had prompted his letter considered with his letter, so that the jury could see the context. The defence was solely fair comment, and the House of Lords decided firstly, that the letter should be considered on its own and secondly, that there should be a retrial as to whether the words complained of were fact or comment. At the subsequent retrial, the statements were held to be fact rather than comment, and Telnikoff was awarded damages of £240,000. (See also Section I, Chapter 1.)

Malice

As a general rule, intent of the defendant is irrelevant. However, in the defences of fair comment and qualified privilege (see Chapter 5), the defence can be defeated if the defendant can be shown to have been actuated by malice, in the legal sense of spite, ill-will or improper motive. The burden of proving malice is on the plaintiff and particulars of the facts in support of the allegations of malice must be given. An example of malice could be where a reviewer of a play has used strong language because the leading actor has eloped with the critic's wife and the critical reviewer has a grudge against the actor. Occasionally a court can be asked to infer malice from the wording of the alleged libel or its accompanying text. If, for example, in a book there are a number of denigrating comments made about the plaintiff as well as the defamatory comments in respect of which he is suing, it may be open to the plaintiff to rely on the denigrating comments as evidence of malice by the defendant. Similarly, where the defendant can be shown not to have believed in the truth of what he published or to be indifferent as to whether the words were true or not, that could be evidence of malice. Malice has been described judicially as difficult to establish but juries can be quick to find malice if there is any evidence of ill-will, rivalry or plainly disruptive behaviour on the part of the defendant.

The defence requires that the expression of comment by the defendant must be his honest view in which he genuinely believes. It follows that if he did not genuinely hold the view expressed (*Merivale v Carson* (1887) 20 QBD 275), or made the statement knowing that it was untrue *Fountain v Boodle* (1842) 3 QB 5), then either of those two situations could be relied upon by the plaintiff as evidence of malice, the onus being on the plaintiff to prove the allegation. In *Vladimir Telnikoff v*

Matusevich above, Mr Telnikoff alleged malice against Mr Matusevich; the defence failed, because on the retrial defamatory statements were held to be statements of fact for which there was no plea of justification, and in respect of which malice was irrelevant.

Example

In *Earl of Stradbroke v Gilbey* (1990), unreported, the Earl of Stradbroke, the colourful father of 14 children, nicknamed 'The Aussie Earl', sued the *Daily Telegraph* and Anthony Gilbey who had written a letter to the *Telegraph* which accused the plaintiff of lying. The dispute arose out of a bitter family dispute within the Stradbroke family and Mr Gilbey claimed that he had written the letter to help redress the reputation of his late father-in-law. It was held that Anthony Gilbey, the writer of the letter, was actuated by malice in writing and so this vitiated his defence plea of fair comment.

In *Johnson v Radio City* (1988), unreported, the case of the French caravan site, the defences included fair comment. Malice was alleged against the defendants on the grounds, *inter alia*, that the disc jockey had omitted from his programme any reference to a number of satisfied holidaymakers, of which he had been aware. The defence failed and the plaintiff was awarded damages of £350,000 (see Section I, Chapter 1).

Practial considerations

It is frequently the case that a defamatory allegation will be made up of statements partly of fact and partly of comment. In this event, it is necessary to plead separately the defence of justification in relation to those statements of fact, and the defence of fair comment in relation to those parts of the words which are alleged to be opinion. On the BBC television quiz show *Have I Got News for You* the word 'allegedly' is commonly inserted before members of the panel make obviously defamatory statements. The use of this word would not prevent the statements from being actionable. It is also important, if advising before publication, to note that the insertion of words such as 'appears', 'apparent' or 'seems' will not usually render a statement of fact an expression of opinion.

In justification, the defendant may rely to the limited extent indicated (see Section II, Chapter 3) on facts which have occurred after the date of the publication complained of, on the basis that the plaintiff is not entitled to recover damages for a reputation to which he is not entitled. However, in the case of fair comment, it is necessary that the facts on which the comment is based should be true at the time the comment is made.

Check list

(1) What are the facts known to your client on which he bases his comment?

(2) Is it his honest opinion and is it such an opinion as could objectively speaking be honestly held having regard to the known facts?

(3) Is he actuated by malice or are there any circumstances whereby the plaintiff could make such an allegation?

(4) Was any consideration given to giving the plaintiff a right of reply?

(5) Is it genuinely a matter of public interest?

(6) Can evidence be obtained to support the facts on which the comment is based?

(7) Were the facts on which the comment is based true at the time of the publication of the alleged libel?

Chapter 5

Privilege

Definition

If the words were published on an occasion protected by privilege, then if that can be established, that is a defence to a libel action. This can apply to both statements of fact and expressions of opinion.

Absolute privilege means that however defamatory, untrue, or malicious, there can be no redress for the plaintiff, because the defamatory statement was published on an occasion of absolute privilege. It is a matter of public policy that there should be certain occasions when persons can be free to speak their mind without fear of a libel action. The occasions when defamatory statements are protected by the plea of absolute privilege are set out below. There are similarly a number of occasions where the defence of privilege will be available to the maker of the statement, but the privilege is qualified on the basis that it can be defeated if the plaintiff can show that the defendant was actuated by malice, in the same legal sense of ill-will, spite or improper motive as can defeat a defence of fair comment.

Absolute privilege

Absolute privilege attaches to publication of defamatory statements if the statements were made on the following occasions:

    (a) judicial proceedings;
    (b) parliamentary proceedings;
    (c) waiver
    (d) reports by either Houses of Parliament;
    (e) quasi-judicial proceedings;
    (f) parliamentary Commissioners' Reports;
    (g) fair and accurate newspaper reports of judicial proceedings;
    (h) documents referred to on any of the above occasions.

No action for libel will lie if a defamatory statement is made in any of the above circumstances. While the onus of proof that the occasion was protected by absolute privilege lies on the defendant, it is a matter of law for the judge to decide whether or not the occasion was so protected. If there is dispute about the facts then the jury, if there is one, will resolve the issues of facts before the matter returns to the judge.

Judicial proceedings

The privilege extends to all statements made in court by the judge, counsel, parties, witnesses or even jurors irrespective of any intent. If a witness in a case should choose to use the opportunity deliberately to defame a third party, that third party will have no recourse in defamation unless the statement is repeated outside the protection of the court.

Example
In the late 1970s the then leader of the Liberal Party, Jeremy Thorpe, was accused of conspiracy to murder the journalist Norman Scott (*R v Thorpe* (1978), unreported), and in the course of the proceedings remarks were made about the distinguished lawyer, the late Lord Goodman. Although Lord Goodman had no legal remedy, exceptionally the court agreed to hear a statement read by a QC instructed by him on the following day in court. Normally such recourse will not be available to a person defamed in court. The statement must, however, be made in the course of the proceedings, so that a gratuitous comment made by a bystander will not be protected (*Delegal v Highley* (1837) 3 Bing NC 950). Similarly, a defamatory statement, perhaps shouted by a witness from the body of the court but while he is not under oath in the witness box, would not be protected.

The recognition of the absolute privilege attaching to the contemporaneous reports of judicial proceedings is now enshrined in s 14 of the Defamation Act 1996. This section also covers those occasions where contemporaneous reporting is prevented under a court order, to avoid risk of prejudice or for other reasons: in such cases publication is protected by absolute privilege provided it is made as soon as practicable after the publication is permitted or the order restricting it expires.

Parliamentary proceedings

Any statements made in either Houses of Parliament are again protected by absolute privilege from proceedings for defamation (*Dillon v Balfur*

(1887) 20 TLR Ir 600). This applies even when the maker of the statement is aware that it is untrue. There have been cases in recent years where highly defamatory allegations about named individuals have been made under the protection of the privilege given to proceedings in Parliament, and even though when challenged the maker of the statement has refused to repeat the defamatory statement outside the protection of the House, there is still no remedy the defamed person can take under the defamation laws. The privilege also extends to statements made under oath to a Select Committee. This privilege is of increasing relevance now that not only proceedings in the Houses of Parliament but also hearings before the Select Committee are televised.

Waiver

Parliamentary privilege dates back to art IX of the Bill of Rights 1689 which was designed to protect MPs so that they could speak freely. The effect of this, however, is that parliamentary debates and proceedings cannot be discussed in court, since this would amount to a breach of parliamentary privilege. This dilemma poses on the one hand, the need for a fair trial in which the evidence in the parliamentary proceedings would be available to defend the proceedings, and on the other hand, the necessity for proceedings in Parliament to be absolutely protected.

Under s 13 of the Defamation Act 1996 it is now open to a member of Parliament to waive the protection of Parliament.

What the section specifies is that where the conduct of a person in relation to proceedings in Parliament is in issue in defamation proceedings, that person may waive for the purposes of those proceedings:

> ... the protection of any enactment or rule of law which prevents proceedings in Parliament being impeached or questioned in any Court or place out of Parliament.

The section goes on to specify where the protection is waived, then questions can be raised about that person's conduct and such questions shall not be regarded as infringing the privilege of the Houses of Parliament. Significantly the waiver by a person of the protection does not affect the operation of that protection in relation to any other person who has not waived the protection. Also, s 13(5) specifically retains absolute privilege in relation to the circumstances set out in that sub-section including, obviously, evidence or statements in either House of Parliament, committee evidence, documentation prepared for a committee, or other communications with a committee of either House. This recognises, as mentioned above, the increasing importance which Select Committees now play in parliamentary life. It will be interesting to see how much this waiver is used in practice. There have been two recent cases where s 13 has been used.

Examples

Absolute privilege arose in an unusual way in respect of libel actions brought in 1995 by the MP Neil Hamilton, a former government minister, and the well-known parliamentary lobbyist, Ian Greer. The *Guardian* had published an article accusing Mr Hamilton of accepting £2,000 in payment from Mohammed Al Fayed, the owner of Harrods, in return for placing parliamentary questions. Mr Greer and his company were accused of offering payments to MPs to ask questions. Both issued proceedings for libel. Since the *Guardian* had repeated allegations made in the House of Commons, the question of parliamentary privilege went before the judge as a preliminary issue. The judge at first instance ruled that to discuss the evidence in the case would breach parliamentary privilege.

The *Guardian* newspaper successfully applied to have the libel actions brought against it stayed, namely stopped on the grounds that the defence would have to investigate the motives and behaviour of MPs. This would be a direct infringement of the parliamentary privilege referred to, that no one can bring into question anything said or done in the House, or imply that actions or words were inspired by improper motive or untrue or misleading. As a result of the implementation of s 13, the action was revived, but abandoned by the plaintiffs the day before the trial on terms which included a payment of £7,500 by each plaintiff.

A similar problem arose with the Tory MP, Rupert Allason, who writes books under the pseudonym Nigel West. He named, in the Houses of Parliament, a journalist who he had alleged had betrayed an Israeli to the Israeli authorities in relation to the alleged leaking of Israeli nuclear secrets. The *Today* newspaper published an article claiming that in making this claim in the House of Commons, the plaintiff had behaved in a cowardly way. In a subsequent article, *Today* claimed that in two early day motions presented by Mr Allason, one in 1991 and one in 1995, the House of Commons had a greater concern to protect MPs named in the early day motions than in the case of the journalist alleged to have betrayed the Israeli mentioned.

Rupert Allason sued for libel, claiming that this meant that he had hidden behind parliamentary privilege and behaved in a cowardly and dishonourable way. *Today* successfully applied to have the proceedings stayed. The basis for the stay was that the matters excluded under the parliamentary privilege were 'the complete essential' for a defence of justification. To refuse a stay would have been unjust to the defendant, but one of the judges stated that he accepted that it was 'a profound denial of justice both to the plaintiff and to the defendant'. Similarly, this action can now be revived should Rupert Allason wish to avail himself of the privilege of waiving parliamentary privilege under s 13 of the 1996 Act.

The owner of Harrods himself, Mr Al Fayed, wrote to the newspapers when he was accused in the House of Commons of blackmail, a statement which was widely reported. No redress was available to Mr Fayed. It is questionable as to whether, even if it consented, the House of Commons has power to waive its privilege, although it is established that *Hansard* can be invoked to establish the meaning of a statute, where an ambiguity is raised, eg *Pepper v Hart* [1993] AC 593, where *Hansard* was invoked to aid statutory construction in a tax case.

Reports by either the House of Commons or the Lords

It follows from the foregoing that the privilege also extends to reports published by order of Parliament from either House.

Quasi-judicial proceedings

The same rationale that gave rise to the protection of absolute privilege in the circumstances outlined, namely that it was contrary to public policy that people should not be free to express the truth, also extends to quasi-judicial proceedings such as tribunals, commissions and enquiries. This is again relevant nowadays because of the increasing use of employment tribunals, and the sometimes sensational reports in cases, for example, of unfair dismissal and sexual or racial harassment.

Parliamentary Commissioners' Reports

There is a special statutory provision under the Parliamentary Commissioner Act 1967 which confirms absolute privilege in any Commissioners' Report or any communication in relation thereto.

Fair and accurate contemporaneous newspaper reports of judicial proceedings

A fair and accurate report of a judicial proceeding if published contemporaneously, is protected by absolute privilege under s 3 of the Law of Libel Amendment Act 1888, which was subsequently limited by the Defamation Act 1952 to fair and accurate reports of courts 'exercising judicial authority within the UK and extending to broadcasts'. To be fair and accurate, the report, even if summarised, should give a balanced view, with no undue emphasis to one side or the other.

Under s 14 of the Defamation Act 1996, the statutory defence of absolute privilege is extended to fair and accurate reports of contemporaneous proceedings in any European Court of Justice Reports, the European Court of Human Rights Reports and any international criminal tribunals established by the Security Council of the United Nations, or by an international agreement to which the UK is a party.

Example

In *Jeffrey Archer v Star* (see above) the prostitute claimed repeatedly in her evidence that Jeffrey Archer had lied, and a number of tabloid newspapers featured on their front page the next day a picture of the prostitute with the large heading 'He lied and lied and lied'. Jeffrey Archer could take no action on these publications because they were protected by absolute privilege.

Documents referred to on any of the above occasions

This is to a large extent self-explanatory, but means that the protection given, for example, in court proceedings to statements made by the judge or any of the parties, would extend to extracts from documents read out in those proceedings, *mutatis mutandis*, or similarly applicable to statements read out in the Houses of Parliament or in quasi-judicial proceedings.

Qualified privilege

The difference between the defence of absolute privilege and qualified privilege is that a plea that the defamatory statement was published on an occasion of qualified privilege can be defeated if the plaintiff can show that the defendant was actuated by malice in the same sense as can vitiate a defence of fair comment. The defence of qualified privilege extends to publication of defamatory statements, providing they were not malicious, if the defamatory statements are made on the following occasions:

    (a) reports of parliamentary proceedings;
    (b) fair and accurate reports of judicial proceedings where not contemporaneous;
    (c) communications made in performance or discharge of a duty to persons who have a like duty or interest in receiving the same;

    (d) communications made for the protection or furtherance of an interest to persons who have a common or corresponding interest in receiving the same;

    (e) statutory reports.

The onus is on the defendant to show that publication occurred on an occasion protected by qualified privilege, and on the plaintiff to show that the defendant acted maliciously.

Reports of parliamentary proceedings

Statements made in either Houses of Parliament are, as we have seen, protected by absolute privilege and reports of those statements are protected by qualified privilege.

Fair and accurate reports of judicial proceedings where not contemporaneous

Fair and accurate reports of court proceedings, where not contemporaneous, are protected by qualified privilege. The test of what is fair and accurate is the same as for absolute privilege, and is particularly relevant for those relying on extracts from trials in writing books.

Examples

In 1996, the Crown Court judge, Judge Griffiths, sued a south coast news agency over a report of his handling of a sexual assault trial. Judge Griffiths had ordered a sex offender to pay £500 to his victim and £950 costs and the news agency report was headlined 'A sex attacker was told by a judge today he would not have been in the dock if he had sent his victim a bunch of flowers'. In the ensuing publicity there was a national furore and women's groups were critical of the judge. However, the report failed to make clear that the victim of the assault had herself said to the judge that she would probably have forgiven her attacker if he had apologised. She had resumed an earlier sexual relationship with the assailant and had sought to have her complaint withdrawn. It was agreed that as the case involved court proceedings, it would be protected by privilege provided it was contemporaneous, accurate and fair. It was accepted that the reports were contemporaneous and accurate but the news agency, by ignoring part of the case, had not been fair and therefore the defence of qualified privilege could not succeed.

An attempt was made to extend the scope of newspaper protection in *Webb v Times Publishing* [1960] 2 QB 535. This case arose out of the report of a murder trial in a Swiss Court. A Mr Hume was stated to have admitted killing Stanley Setty and the report was headlined 'Body dismembered and thrown from aircraft'. The article went on to state that Hume claimed that his child was fathered by Stanley Setty. Hume's wife, who had never met Setty and had given evidence to that effect at an earlier trial in England, sued *The Times* newspaper for libel claiming that the report meant that she had committed adultery with Setty and had given perjured evidence at Hume's trial in 1950. *The Times* claimed that as it was a contemporaneous report, it was protected by qualified privilege as it was a fair and accurate report of foreign judicial proceedings. It was held that the report could be protected because the subject matter of the report was a legitimate and proper interest to the English reader because it was connected with the administration of justice in England and the reference to the father of the child being Stanley Setty explained an alleged motive of jealousy.

The Scott Report into the 'arms to Iraq affair' was an example of a report protected by qualified privilege under the Schedule to the Defamation Act 1952.

Communications made in discharge of a duty

Communications made in performance or discharge of a duty to persons who have a like duty or interest in receiving the same covers, for example, statements made by an employer to a prospective employer regarding a reference for an employee. The duty can be legal or moral or simply a social one. It would in addition cover statements made to the police about suspected crime. This would cover private statements where a public statement would be protected by statutory privilege. The statement must be made by the person who has a duty to make it and the protection of qualified privilege only extends to its publication to the person who has a corresponding duty or interest in receiving that statement. If the defamatory statement is published to persons who have no such interest or duty, then the defence will usually fail. The defence can be defeated as in fair comment, if the plaintiff is able to show that the defendant acted maliciously.

Examples

In *Welsh v Transport and General Workers Union* (1991), unreported, there was a defamatory allegation that the plaintiff, James Welsh, had stolen and misused union funds. This allegation was published in the newsletter of the Transport and General Workers Union. It was claimed that the publication was to members only and was published on an occasion of qualified privilege. However, two of the four defendants were found to have acted maliciously and the plaintiff was awarded £100,000 damages.

Privilege could also extend to an employer giving an account of reasons for dismissal of an employee to his remaining employees (*Hunt v Great Northern Railway* [1891] 2 QB 189 CA).

In *Buckingham v Dove and Rusk* (1994), unreported, the plaintiff was an amateur golfer; the two defendants were members of his golf club who had independently reported him to the club committee for two separate incidents of alleged cheating. The golf club committee investigated, found that the facts were not proved and the matter was closed. Mr Buckingham however chose to pursue his fellow members through the libel courts. The defendants pleaded qualified privilege on the grounds that they had a duty to make the report to the club and the club committee had a corresponding interest in receiving it. An allegation of malice was made but the jury found for the defendants and left the plaintiff to pick up a very substantial bill of costs.

One consequence of the action, which is an unfortunate result of the considerable publicity given to libel actions, is that the original libel, known only to a few members of the plaintiff's golf club, was then front page news on almost every national newspaper, with the plaintiff's reputation damaged by further evidence of incidents of cheating on the golf course given at the trial.

An untested case of qualified privilege arose in *WPC Robson v Flood* (1992), unreported. In that case the facts were that the defendant's car was clamped under the supervision of WPC Robson. The defendant wrote to her employers demanding that the fine and the unclamping fee be returned and made offensive remarks about WPC Robson in his letter. The money was subsequently refunded to Mr Flood, who withdrew his complaint against WPC Robson. However, she won the financial backing from the Police Federation to sue for libel and Mr Flood, unable to get legal aid, settled out of court for £500 damages. Had the matter gone to trial, Mr Flood's letter of complaint could have been protected by the defence of qualified privilege, and it would have been necessary for the plaintiff to prove malice in court to defeat any such defence.

A potential problem relating to qualified privilege arose over a recent crime prevention initiative against street prostitutes. Police officers in the Tottenham area of London had been filming cars picking up prostitutes and were reported to be planning to send video stills of the car numbers to the registered owners. In 20 to 30 per cent of cases, this would be the employer. The implication that the employee had solicited a prostitute could be defamatory, and it might be hard to claim that there was sufficient duty or interest in the employer being informed of this unless there were restrictions on how the vehicle was to be used, for example, business use only.

Communications for the protection of interested parties

This would cover cases where, for example, shareholders in a company were informed of matter relating to the company. In *James Roland-Jones v City and Westminster Financial plc* (1990), unreported, the defamatory statement was circulated not only to shareholders but also to members of the Stock Exchange. It was held that the circulation to members of the Stock Exchange was too wide and the defence of qualified privilege failed. A contrast is provided by *Adam v Ward* [1917] AC 309. In that case, the plaintiff, who was a member of Parliament, made criticisms of a general under whose command he had been when he had been a cavalry officer and claimed that the general's confidential reports to headquarters were full of untruths. The matter was referred to the Army Council for their investigation and on the direction of the Council, the secretary, who was the defendant, wrote a letter to the general exonerating him from the charges but also making defamatory statements about the plaintiff. Copies were circulated to MPs and to the press for publication. The letter was widely publicised, the plaintiff sued for libel and the defence of qualified privilege was pleaded. It was held by the House of Lords that as the original speech by the plaintiff in the House of Commons had been widely reported, the publication by the defendant did not go beyond what was acceptable and the defence of qualified privilege could be appropriate.

Any claim for libel based on an employee's reference is, of course, completely distinct from any claim for damages in negligence if an employer failed to take reasonable care in preparing a reference.

Examples

Spring v Guardian Assurance plc [1994] IRLR 460, HL restated the principles of qualified privilege. Qualified privilege attaches to letters sent by former employers to prospective employers, but if the disgruntled employee who is complaining that the reference is defamatory is unable to prove malice, he may still succeed if he can show negligence in the sense of carelessness on the part of his former employer rather than recklessness in the preparation of the reference. This situation arose in 1995 when a Michelle Brenton had a job offer withdrawn, following what she alleged was an incorrect reference about her given by the Polytechnic of Wales where she had been a student. She issued proceedings not for defamation, but for negligence and accepted the sum of £25,000 in settlement.

It is easier for a plaintiff to succeed in establishing negligent misstatement than to establish malice in libel or slander, as the standard of proof required is lower. Disgruntled employees would be well advised to sue for negligent misstatement therefore; firstly because it is easier to prove carelessness than recklessness (which is a component of malice) and secondly, the need in a libel action to plead the precise terms of the reference of which the employee may not have a copy, as opposed to relying on the gist of the reference in negligent misstatement.

Statutory reports

Statutory protection for publication of certain reports by public bodies, is given under s 15 of the Defamation Act 1952.

Example

An interesting extension was given to the protection of newspapers in the case of *Tsikata v Newspaper Publishing plc* (1994) *The Times*, 9 November. The facts of that case arose out of serious allegations about human rights in Ghana under the military regime. After the overthrow of the civilian government by the military in 1981, a special investigation board was set up by the Ghanaian government to conduct an enquiry into the murders in 1982 of three Ghanaian High Court judges. In its conclusion, the report held that the murders had been masterminded by a Captain Tsikata, who brought proceedings in the UK for defamation over an article repeating the findings of the report. It was not disputed that the article reported the findings of the Board accurately, and it was held as a preliminary issue that the question was not whether the Board's findings and recommendations were themselves fair or accurate, but whether the report for which qualified privilege was obtained, was itself fair and accurate. The newspaper's defence was that the defence of qualified privilege applied, as its article was protected as a publication of the findings of a public body under the statutory privilege for newspapers provided for in s 7 of the Defamation Act 1952. It was held that the defence of qualified privilege could apply.

One of the important additions to the Schedule to the Defamation Act 1996 is that the protection which previously extended only to newspapers sold for payment is now extended to 'reports'; this means that the protection of the Schedule extends to free newspapers, and other publications, a welcome extension.

An interesting attempt to extend the scope of qualified privilege arose in *Watts v Times Newspapers Ltd (Schilling & Lom, a firm)* [1996] 1 All ER 152.

Example

In that case the *Sunday Times* had published a story in two places in the paper: as a diary item and as a longer piece elsewhere. Both articles alleged that the plaintiff author had plagiarised somebody else's work, and as a result had dishonestly obtained a literary prize. Inadvertently, the article was accompanied by a photograph of a property developer of the same name. The newspaper subsequently published a detailed letter from the plaintiff author denying the allegation of plagiarism.

Solicitors however, representing the property developer claimed that he had been defamed and the newspaper published an apology which included, at his solicitors' insistence, a further reference to the allegation of plagiarism against the plaintiff. The plaintiff author then issued libel proceedings in respect of the original article and the apology. The newspaper pleaded qualified privilege and sought to join the property developer's lawyers, Schilling and Lom, to the proceedings as a third party.

As a preliminary issue, it was held at first instance that the apology was not protected by qualified privilege. On appeal, it was held firstly, that the newspaper and the solicitors were in a different situation in relation to qualified privilege; secondly, that it was not open to the newspaper to rely on the defence of qualified privilege, since their obligation to apologise to the property developer did not justify the inclusion in the apology of a further attack on the plaintiff author which undermined the letter from him recently published; and thirdly, in relation to the solicitors, it was held that the circumstances surrounding the publication of an apology did amount to an occasion of qualified privilege, and since there was no allegation of malice the third party proceedings should be struck out against the solicitors.

Malice

The defence of qualified privilege can be defeated if the plaintiff can prove that the defendant was actuated by malice, in the same legal sense as for fair comment, namely spite, ill-will or improper motive. See *Buckingham v Dove and Rusk* above.

Check list

(1) Can it be clearly established that publication was on a privileged occasion?

(2) If it was on a privileged occasion, is it an occasion of absolute privilege or qualified privilege?

(3) In relation to qualified privilege, was there a duty or interest between the maker and the receiver of the statement?

(4) Is the publication too wide for qualified privilege to apply?

(5) Is publication of the report protected by Sched 1, Pt I or Pt II to the Defamation Act 1996?

(6) If Pt II, has a request for a letter to be published by way of explanation or contradiction been received, and has the letter been published?

(7) In relation to a defence of qualified privilege can any allegation of malice be made by the plaintiff?

(8) Are there any facts from which the court could infer malice?

Chapter 6

Unintentional Defamation

This statutory defence of an offer of amends under s 4 of the Defamation Act 1952, now simplified under ss 2–4 of the Defamation Act 1996, was designed to give a defendant protection where there had been a genuine mistake or the innocent misuse of another's name. Although the provision was enacted to cover a *lacuna* in the then existing law, it has not been widely used in practice but the amended offer of amends procedure in the new Act should lead to its wider use.

Application

The defence can apply to both statements of fact and expressions of opinion, provided they are published as a result of an innocent mistake and provided those publishing the statement have taken all reasonable care.

Examples
An example of the problems which it was designed to alleviate occurred in *Hulton v Jones* [1909] 2 KB 444, CA, and a similar situation arose in *Newstead v London Express* [1940] 1 KB 377. (See Section I, Chapter 1.)

The defence of an offer of amends under s 4 of the Defamation Act 1952 and now ss 2–4 of the Defamation Act 1996 provides a defence in these situations as well as in the *Cassidy v Daily Mirror* [1929] 2 KB 331 type actions also referred to in Section I, Chapter 1.

This defence could also have been appropriate providing there was reasonable care when *The Times* printed an article about the financial ruin of the gambler and former owner of Harrods, Hugh Fraser, which was unfortunately accompanied by a photograph of the highly respectable Tory MP, Sir Hugh Fraser, who settled for damages of £10,000.

Offer of amends

In order to establish the defence under s 4 of the Defamation Act 1952, the defendant had to prove:

  (a) that the words were published innocently of and concerning the plaintiff;
  (b) that he had made an offer of amends which had to include the withdrawal of offending material and a method of making a suitable correction and sufficient apology available to those to whom the original libel was likely to have been distributed; and
  (c) that the offer of amends was refused by the plaintiff and was still available at trial.

The offer was normally worded in the same way as set out in the Act. If the offer was accepted the proceedings came to an end, although the suitable correction and apology had to be agreed; if the parties could not agree, the court could be asked to decide the wording of the correction and apology.

The offer of amends under ss 2–4 of the Defamation Act 1996 must be made in writing, must be expressed to be an offer under s 2 of the Act and must state whether it is a qualified offer (see below). The offer is to:

  (a) make a suitable correction and apology;
  (b) publish the correction and apology in a manner which is reasonable and practicable;
  (c) pay the aggrieved party such compensation (if any) and such costs as may be agreed or determined to be payable.

If the offer is accepted by the plaintiff then that is the end to the proceedings. If, however, the parties cannot agree on the correction, apology and publication, then the correction and apology can be done by way of a statement in open court with an undertaking as to publication. Similarly, if the parties cannot agree on compensation or costs these also shall be determined by the court. The court is in fact a judge alone, with no provision for a jury.

Under s 4 of the Act, if an offer is made and not withdrawn and not accepted, then it is a defence to the libel proceedings. It is essential for it to operate as a defence that the person on whose behalf the offer is made, must not have known that the statement complained of referred to the plaintiff or was likely to be understood as referring to him or that it was false or defamatory of the plaintiff. An important distinction from the previous Act is that there is now a presumption that that is the case until the contrary is shown. Therefore, the burden of showing that the defendant did know that the words could be understood to refer to the plaintiff and were false and defamatory of him shifts to the plaintiff.

An important additional provision under s 4 is that a qualified offer can be made. This means that where part of the alleged defamatory material has been published innocently, an offer of amends could be made in respect of that part but leaving the defendant open to pursue another defence in respect of other parts of the material. If the offer of amends is accepted, that is an end to the proceedings. If it is not accepted it can be relied on as a defence but if so no other defence may be relied on.

Finally, if the offer is not accepted and the defendant relies on some other defences, the offer of amends can be relied on in mitigation.

Innocence

Under s 4 of the Defamation Act 1952, it was necessary for a defendant to show that he had exercised all reasonable care and that the offer had been made as soon as practicable. To show innocence, the publisher had to swear an affidavit in support of the offer of amends, in which he had to show, either that he did not intend to publish the words complained of, concerning the plaintiff, and did not know of circumstances in which they might be understood to refer to him (*Newstead v London Express*, above), or that the words were not defamatory on the face of them, and that he did not know of circumstances by virtue of which they might be understood to be defamatory of the plaintiff (*Cassidy v Daily Mirror* above). Only the facts set out in the defendant's affidavit sworn in support of the offer could be relied upon at the trial, so that all relevant material had to be included.

In both cases, the publisher, irrespective of whether he was also the author, had to show that he had exercised all reasonable care. In the affidavit therefore, it was necessary to set out what checks, for example, of telephone directories or trade directories, were made before publication. In addition, where the publisher was not the author, the publisher had to show that the author was not actuated by malice.

In order to operate as a defence, the defendant had to file the affidavit and the offer of amends, which had to be made 'as soon as practicable after the defendant received notice' that the words were or might be defamatory of the plaintiff. This placed a considerable burden on the defendant, who had to assemble all his evidence and incorporate it in an affidavit very quickly.

In contrast, the new offer of amends defence in the 1996 Act allows the defendant to make an offer at any time up until service of defence. In affording the defendant more time to investigate the circumstances surrounding the publication complained of, and the possibility of justifying or otherwise defending the action, the new offer of amends defence is likely to be more useful than the previous 1952 defence to a defendant, particularly with the presumption of innocence now in the defendant's favour.

Example
In the leading case of *Ross v Hopkinson* (1956) *The Times*, 17 October it was held that an offer made within seven weeks was not made 'as soon as practicable'. In that case a novel included a character called June Sylvane who was described in uncomplimentary terms. She was depicted as a minor actress, aged 20 at York Repertory Theatre. A real actress of the same name, aged 20 at York Repertory Theatre, sued the author, publishers and printers for libel. They maintained that the libel was unintentional and that they had made a suitable offer of amends under s 4. It was held that the offer was made too late, although only seven weeks elapsed between the publishers being notified of the libel and making the offer of amends. In addition, it was held that the publishers, which included the author, had not taken all reasonable care as no checks had been made in the local *Variety* or telephone directory in the York area.

Correction

The offer itself is an offer to publish or join in the publication of a suitable correction and a sufficient apology and to take such steps as are reasonably practical to notify those to whom copies have been distributed. In the case of a book, the notification can be dealt with by way of, for example, a notice in the *Bookseller*. One reason why the offer of amends under the Defamation Act 1952 was not widely used in practice was that the section related to 'innocent' defamation. After notification of alleged libel, further distribution could not be innocent, so effectively distribution of a book, for example, had to cease.

Under s 2 of the Defamation Act 1996, the offer is to publish a correction and apology in a manner that is both 'reasonable and practicable in the circumstances'. Section 3 contains a provision that if the parties cannot agree on the apology, the plaintiff may have a statement in open court.

Example
In *Campbell v BBC* (1990), unreported, the investigative journalist, Duncan Campbell, accepted £50,000 agreed damages from the BBC over a play featuring an investigative journalist. The journalist in the play was called David Dunhill and was portrayed as a journalist who abandoned his sources, was a transvestite and a shoplifter. Although the origi-

nal character had been depicted by the writer of the play as aged 50, the BBC drama department had chosen a younger actor of similar age and build to Mr Campbell, had used pictures of his flat and even shot scenes in the supermarket where he shopped. It was claimed there were 17 major resemblances to him. In view of this there could be no possibility of the BBC relying on the defence of innocent defamation as the publishers would not have been able to show that they had taken all reasonable care.

Summary of offer of amends under the Defamation Act 1996

Under ss 2–4 of the Defamation Act 1996, the offer to make amends is preserved with certain important differences:
  (a) the offer now includes payment of damages;
  (b) there is no requirement that the offer should be made 'as soon as practicable', although it must be made before service of defence;
  (c) there is no requirement that, where the publisher is not the author, he can only rely on the defence if he proves that the author wrote the words without malice. This was always a difficulty for publishers and its removal is welcomed;
  (d) there is provision for a qualified offer. In other words, where an innocent mistake relates to only part of the article complained of, an offer of amends can be made in respect of that part;
  (e) if the offer is relied on as a defence, no other defence may be relied on but it can be relied on in mitigation;
  (f) if the offer is accepted it is an end to the proceedings subject to the right of the court to approve the apology, have a statement in open court and determine the compensation and costs if not agreed as mentioned above.

The changes which are beneficial to a plaintiff are that the offer includes compensation. The changes that are beneficial to a defendant are:
  (a) the removal of the strict time limit;
  (b) the presumption of innocence; and
  (c) the provision for a qualified offer.

It may, however, prove unattractive for a defendant to rely on the offer of amends as a defence, as the Act precludes relying on any other defence. It may be in practice that an offer of amends, if made and rejected, will be relied on in mitigation only, with other substantive defences pleaded as may be appropriate.

Check list

(1) Is the defendant willing to make an offer of amends which will include a correction, publication of the correction and payment of compensation to be decided by the court in the absence of agreement?

(2) Is the offer of amends to relate to all the alleged defamatory allegations or is it to be a qualified offer?

(3) Does the defendant realise that if the offer is made and not accepted, it can be relied upon as a defence but no other defence can be relied on?

(4) Does the defendant wish to make an offer but rely on it in mitigation and put other defences in?

(5) Is it clear that the defendant did not know that the alleged defamatory material could refer, or was likely to be understood to refer to the plaintiff, and that it was false and defamatory of the plaintiff?

Chapter 7

Other Defences

In this chapter, further defences are considered, with other matters, which although not a defence, may assist a defendant.

Consent

This defence is known also as *volenti non fit injuria* or leave and licence. It means that if the plaintiff has consented to publication of defamatory statements and the defendant can prove that consent, that is a complete defence to a libel action.

Application

This defence frequently arises when a newspaper report or television broadcast occurs as a result of an interview with the plaintiff. Putting defamatory statements to a plaintiff, which he then rebuts, does not amount to consent to publication of the defamatory statements. If the plaintiff does consent to publication but the publication is to a wider audience or not substantially the same as that to which the plaintiff consented, then the defence may fail.

Example

An attempt to run this defence failed at first instance in *Anthony Gilberthorpe v News Group Newspapers* (1989) 139 New LJ 1039. In that case libel action was brought by a Gloucester councillor in respect of an article in which he was quoted as saying that he would resign because of allegations that he was being treated for AIDS. A defence of leave and licence was filed on the basis that the article arose out of a telephone call by the plaintiff to a reporter of a local news agency, which then passed the information to other newspapers. The plaintiff recovered £9,750 damages against the *Daily Mirror*, £9,750 against the local paper and £28,750 against the *Sun*. He denied that he had spoken to the reporter or that he was a homosexual. Later statements were placed before the Court of Appeal confirming that the plaintiff was a homosexual. The court ordered a retrial where other defences might be open to the defendants as well as the defence of leave and licence. Subsequently an application was made in 1995 by the defendants to strike the case out for want of prosecution but the application failed because the plaintiff said that he had been ill and had been without means (see below). The matter was subsequently settled.

Evidence

Evidence of consent should be clear: if in writing, it might be straightforward to establish. If oral, it should be in front of a witness. However, if there is a dispute as to what was said, a jury may take the word of the plaintiff over two or even three reporters.

Example

In *Moore v News of the World* (1971) *The Times*, 12 May three reporters gave evidence that the plaintiff, Dorothy Squires, then married to the actor, Roger Moore, had consented to publication and had said all the statements of which she complained. Nonetheless the jury believed the plaintiff, who denied that she had spoken as alleged and she was awarded damages.

Accord and satisfaction

If the defendant can prove that the plaintiff has agreed in writing, either under seal (this means in a deed which is irrevocable) to release the defendant, or the defendant has given valuable consideration accepted by the plaintiff, then that is a defence to any libel proceedings. Valuable consideration means that there must be benefit to the party receiving the consideration. The basis for this defence is that there has been a binding contractual agreement between the parties. If, for example, the plaintiff should require a written apology as his only condition of settlement and that written apology is provided, that can be a good defence to an action.

As with consent, the difficulty can arise in establishing the agreement. For example, the plaintiff and defendant discuss the matter over the telephone, and the defendant offers to provide an apology which the plaintiff agrees to accept in final settlement; however, after the apology is provided, the plaintiff commences defamation proceedings and denies the conversation. It would then devolve into an evidential point as to which of the witnesses the jury chooses to believe. Clearly, any such oral agreements should be backed up in writing as soon as possible by the defendant.

Mitigation

It may happen that there is no substantive defence to a libel action and the nominal defences cannot succeed. In that case it may be open to the defendant to plead in mitigation:

    (a)   that the offending publication was withdrawn as soon as notification of the alleged libel was given;

    (b)   that steps were taken to notify persons to whom it had been published that the publication contained an alleged defamatory statement;

    (c)   that an apology was promptly published;

    (d)   that the plaintiff had no reputation which could be damaged;

    (e)   that the plaintiff delayed for a considerable time before bringing proceedings;

    (f)   that the offending publication was only published to a very limited number of people; and

    (g)   that the offending publication was only published to persons who would not have thought any less of the plaintiff or not believed the allegation.

If after notification of the alleged libel, the defendant publishes an apology, whether or not it has been agreed, this can be relied on in mitigation. There is a provision under s 2 of the Libel Act 1843 (popularly known as Lord Campbell's Libel Act), relating specifically to newspapers. It states that provided the defendant newspaper can show that::

    (a)   the alleged libel was published without malice;

    (b)   the alleged libel was published without gross negligence; and

    (c)   the defendants had inserted a full apology;

then coupled with a payment into court this can operate as a complete defence. However, this is a remedy which is very rarely used.

Prior publication of similar words about which the plaintiff has chosen not to take action cannot normally be pleaded in mitigation neither is it possible to claim the publication, the subject matter of the action, has not tarnished the plaintiff's reputation because previous publications have already lowered it.

Examples

The case of *Associated Newspapers v Dingle* [1964] AC 371 arose out of a letter written by a town clerk to shareholders of a cemetery company offering, on behalf of a Manchester corporation, to purchase the shares at £1 each. Subsequently, a report of a House of Commons' Select Committee was published which stated that the Manchester town clerk, the plaintiff in the libel action, had not given the true break-up value of the shares. Publication of that report was absolutely privileged under the Parliamentary Papers Act 1840. However, in an article, the *Daily Mail* published an interview with the chairman of the cemetery company together with reproduction of an extract from the report. The chairman was reported as stating that the shares were worth more than double the amount paid for them by the corporation. The plaintiff sued for libel. Other newspapers' extracts of the Select Committee's report were admitted in evidence to destroy the allegation of malice and in mitigation. Damages of £1,100 were increased by the Court of Appeal to £4,000, *inter alia*, on the basis that a defendant who failed to justify his defamatory statements could not mitigate damages by producing evidence of other publications to the same effect as the libel.

In *Kiam v Neil and Times Newspapers Ltd* (1994) *The Times*, 14 December an attempt by the defence to put before the jury a specific figure offered by way of damages in open correspondence to the plaintiff failed. The judge held that a defendant in a libel action could not be permitted to do this, since otherwise it would always be open to a defendant to make an offer, thus circumventing the rules prohibiting specific figures being canvassed in order to avoid a 'libel auction' where counsel for both parties put differing amounts before the jury. However, this ruling has been impliedly amended by *Elton John v MGN* [1996] 2 All ER 35 (see Section III, Chapter 9).

If an apology is going to be relied upon it is important to consider the prominence of the original article and the prominence of an apology. Frequently a prominent article on page one in large type may have an apology which appears at the bottom of page 15 in small type. Similarly, in negotiations with television apologies, it is prudent to insist that the apology is transmitted at a similar time as the original programme and be read without undue emphasis, which could diminish the effect of the apology. The promptness of an apology is important if it is to be relied on in mitigation as, it will obviously carry more weight with the jury if it was published shortly after the complaint was made rather than as frequently happens, some 18 months after the complaint but two weeks before the trial. Similarly, consideration needs to be given as to the format of the apology whether it should have the name of the plaintiff, whether it should be accompanied by a photograph or whether it should have the word 'apology'. Examples are given in Section IV, Chapter 10.

Statute of limitation

Any claim for libel is barred three years after last publication by the Limitation Act 1980. However, under s 5 of the Defamation Act 1996 the limitation period has been shortened to one year from the date on which the cause of action accrued, namely the date of publication. However, the section does contain a number of provisions for discretionary waiver of the time limit for actions for defamation. This is important since, for example, doctors or policemen, who may be subject to disciplinary proceedings, may not be able to issue a writ for libel until those disciplinary proceedings are concluded. The factors that a court may take into account are the length and reason for the delay on the part of the plaintiff; the fact that the plaintiff did not become aware of the alleged libel until after the end of the limitation period and the extent to which the delay has reduced the availability of relevant evidence (see also Section V, Chapter 11).

Examples

In *Oyston v Blaker* (1995) *The Times*, 15 November the millionaire, Owen Oyston, sought leave to bring proceedings for libel outside the time limit and made an application to the court *ex parte*. Although the judge has a wide discretion in considering whether or not to grant leave to enable a plaintiff to bring libel proceedings outside the time limit, it is essential that the defendant should be heard when such an application is made. It was held on a proper interpretation of RSC, Ord 32, r 9(3), that such an application had to be made by originating summons on notice to the other party. The *ex parte* application therefore failed.

As has been seen earlier (Section I, Chapter 1), in certain slander actions proceedings may only be brought if special damage can be proved. In those cases, the limitation period runs from the date the special damage was sustained since prior to that no cause of action would have arisen. Section 32A of the Limitation Act 1980, as amended by s 57 of the Administration of Justice Act 1985, extends this; if a proposed plaintiff in such an action has not brought the proceedings within the period of three years, because all or any of the relevant facts were not known to him, he may, with the leave of the court, bring proceedings for defamation at any time before the expiry of one year from the earliest date on which he knows all the relevant facts. However, the terms of this section are specific; the three-year time period will only be extended where the plaintiff learns of the relevant facts after this three-year time period has already expired.

Even where the original claim may be statute-barred, if there is any republication proceedings can nonetheless be instituted, since repetition of a libel constitutes a new cause of action, which can be the subject of separate proceedings.

Esample

In *Duke of Brunswick v Harmer* (1849) 14 QB 185 the plaintiff sent his servant to purchase a back copy of a newspaper containing a libel on him which had been published 17 years earlier and which was statute-barred. It was held that such a sale constituted a fresh publication which was not statute-barred. A more recent example occurred when Princess Elizabeth of Toro of Uganda brought proceedings for libel against six English newspapers in the 1980s which had reprinted scurrilous allegations against her by the late Idi Amin, then dictator of Uganda. Each publication gave rise to a fresh cause of action.

In dealing with the repetition of a libel, an interesting case arose in 1995. The facts were that HarperCollins had published an autobiography of cricketer Ian Botham, in which he recounted being arrested and charged for possession of cannabis. The book contained criticism of the way two named police officers had questioned his wife. The police officers issued proceedings for libel and the matter was settled on the basis of undisclosed damages and an undertaking not to repeat the libel in any future editions of the book. Unfortunately, due to 'human error' the paperback, when published later in the year, did contain the alleged libel. It was a repetition of the libel and the two police officers, who immediately and understandably complained again, received what was described as a 'larger additional sum in damages'.

In *Popplewell v Today and INS News Agency* (1992), unreported, proceedings for libel were issued by a judge over a report of proceedings in Reading Crown Court in which he was presiding. Both the news agency which supplied the story to the national press and *Today* newspaper, which ran the story, were sued for libel. The matter was later settled by agreed arbitration before Lord Williams, the libel QC, the first libel case to do so, for payment of £7,500 damages.

An interesting problem in relation to limitation arose out of matrimonial proceedings in *C v Mirror Group Newspapers* (1996) *The Times*, 15 July. In 1988 during the course of a custody dispute, a father made highly defamatory allegations about his wife alleging she had been involved in drug smuggling. The statements, which were made outside the court, were reported in the *Daily Mirror.* Although the allegations were later withdrawn, the wife, who was the plaintiff, resident in Australia, telephoned the newspaper in England to complain about the article and was told that the newspaper was just repeating what her husband had said in court.

In 1993, she received confirmation from the judge that the allegations had not been made in court and in 1994, the plaintiff issued writs for libel and malicious falsehood. The plaintiff claimed in the High Court and in the Court of Appeal that she was not aware until the judge's letter in 1993 that the allegation that she had been involved in drug smuggling had not been made in court. Until then she claimed to have believed that the newspaper reports were privileged as they were accounts of court proceedings. It was held that these were not matters within the exceptions of s 32A of the Limitation Act 1980 (preserved in s 5(4) of the Defamation Act 1996). The plaintiff therefore failed in her application to bring proceedings for libel as she was out of time but she was allowed to continue her proceedings for malicious falsehood.

Innocent dissemination

In the case of a libel, all those responsible for publication, namely the author, reporter, editor, newspaper proprietor and printer, can be sued for libel. Disseminators such as wholesalers, distributors or libraries, usually have a defence of innocent dissemination.

Example

In *Vizetelly v Mudie's Select Library Ltd* [1900] 2 QB 170, CA, a libel action was brought against the library company, Mudie, claiming damages for libel contained in a book circulated by the library. The library successfully established that it had no knowledge that the work contained defamatory matter and the elements of the innocent dissemination defence were laid down, namely that the defendant had to show:

(a) that he had no knowledge of the libel;

(b) there was no reason for him to suppose that the work concerned contained a libel; and

(c) that he had not been negligent in not knowing there was a libel when he disseminated the work.

Once a bookshop, vendor or distributor has been notified that a particular publication contains an alleged libel, however, he is no longer an innocent disseminator and therefore if he continues to distribute, he can be sued for damages for libel in the same way as the original publisher.

Examples

In 1993, the Prime Minister, John Major and the Downing Street cook, Clare Latimer, issued separate proceedings for libel against the *New Statesman* and the now defunct satirical magazine *Scallywag*. The distributors were notified immediately of the alleged libel, and although the two magazines tried to fight the action, the distributors negotiated settlements for which they were indemnified by the magazines. The matter was eventually settled for payment of only £1,001 by the *New Statesman* and no damages by *Scallywag* to the plaintiffs.

Similarly, the technique employed by the late publishing tycoon Robert Maxwell, when he alleged that he had been libelled in Tom Bower's biography of him, *The Outsider*, was to notify all the bookshops stocking the book, after he had issued a writ for libel, that he had done so. This meant that their defence of innocent dissemination was immediately destroyed since they had been notified that the book contained an alleged libel. It is an important weapon in the plaintiff's armour where magazines or books are involved, to see that the distributors' defence is destroyed in this way, as it can then put financial pressure on the publishers to settle because the publishers normally give indemnities in defamation actions to distributors, wholesalers and bookshops.

Under s 1 of the 1996 Act, there is a defence of innocent dissemination if a person can show that he was not 'primarily responsible' for the publication of the statement complained of and that he neither knew nor had any reason to suspect, having taken all reasonable care, that his acts 'involved or contributed' to the publication of the defamatory statement. This was also designed to deal with Internet cases (see Section V, Chapter 11). The section defines the author, editor and publisher as being primarily responsible for publication. Section 1(3) also sets out the categories of persons who will not be regarded as primarily responsible. These broadly amount to the printer, anyone processing or operating electronic equipment or service of distribution and retrieval in electronic form, a broadcaster of an unrecorded statement (this would cover the television news case mentioned earlier, Section I, Chapter 1), and the operator of a communications network; however, these categories are not exhaustive.

This would appear to provide a defence in cases which are just starting to emerge arising from the Internet communications network. However, since the wording of the section is: 'a person has a defence if he shows that ...', the burden of proof still remains on the defendant.

The scale and nature of modern publishing and distribution make this an attractive and highly relevant defence.

Death

In the English courts, if either party to a libel or slander action dies, the action ceases. If a plaintiff in a libel action should die at any time up to and during the trial, the action will completely cease. Similarly, if a defendant dies the plaintiff cannot continue the action against his estate but if, for example, an author and publisher were joint defendants and the author died, the action could continue against the publisher. There is no right either for the plaintiff's personal representatives to continue the proceedings or for personal representatives of the defendant to continue to defend those proceedings.

This is to be contrasted with an action such as infringement of copyright,where a copyright is an asset that can be bequeathed in a will, and the personal representatives or beneficiary can continue an action for infringement of copyright. However, the general principle, *actio personalis moritur cum persona*, namely that the cause of action dies with the person does not apply in many European countries and parts of the US, so care should be taken by publishers or newspapers syndicating material with any indemnities given to foreign publishers.

Example

In Hockhuth's play *The Soldiers*, Sir Winston Churchill was accused of being involved in the murder of the Polish General Sikorski; there was no redress in this country that the family of the late Sir Winston Churchill could take.

The boxer, Terry Marsh, was unsuccessfully prosecuted for the alleged attempted murder of his former promoter, Frank Warren. It was claimed by the prosecution that Terry Marsh's motive in allegedly shooting Frank Warren was to stop the libel action he had brought against Terry Marsh. Terry Marsh was acquitted of murder, and Frank Warren subsequently lost his libel action against him.

General bad reputation

The purpose of a libel action is to obtain recompense for damage to reputation. It is therefore open to the defendant to claim in mitigation that the plaintiff's reputation is already bad. This is done by pleading particulars of reputation in the defence.

Examples

In *Goody v Odhams Press Ltd* [1967] 1 QB 333 one of the Great Train Robbers sued the *People* newspaper over an article which referred to him as one of the Great Train Robbers and stated that he was now in prison for 30 years for his part in the robbery. It was held by the Court of Appeal, on a preliminary issue, that the defendants were entitled to rely in their pleadings on eight previous convictions of the plaintiff in mitigation.

The general rule was established in *Scott v Sampson* (1882) 8 QBD 491 where the question of admissibility of evidence of bad reputation in mitigation of damages was fully considered. The rule may be expressed as follows: that evidence of general bad reputation is admissible but evidence of rumours that the plaintiff has done what was charged in the libel or evidence of particular acts of misconduct on the part of the plaintiff tending to show his character and disposition, could not be adduced.

In *Wood v Cox* (1888) 4 TLR 652 the plaintiff, who was a jockey, brought a libel action over a statement that he had pulled a particular horse on two specified occasions, evidence in mitigation was brought of the plaintiff's general bad reputation for pulling horses.

Where such evidence is given it is, of course, open to the plaintiff to rebut it.

It was hoped that the rule in *Scott v Sampson* would be abolished by the Defamation Act 1996 so that evidence of specific acts could be given but this amendment, originally in the Bill, was not included in the Defamation Act 1996 so the rule in *Scott v Sampson* remains the present position.

Jest or vulgar abuse

In a slander action there is a defence that the words were mere vulgar abuse. There have been occasions where an attempt has been made to rely on a similar type of defence in a libel action, though this is necessarily a high risk strategy. 'If a man in jest can raise a serious imputation he jests at his peril', Judge B Smith in *Donoghue v Hayes* (1831) Hayes (Ir Ex) R p 266.

Examples

An attempt to run such a defence in a libel action was made in *Beloff v Pressdram* [1973] 1 All ER 241. In that case, *Private Eye* had published a satirical article highly defamatory of the journalist Miss Nora Beloff in that it implied that she would prostitute herself to obtain political information. It was contended on behalf of *Private Eye* that the words were jest and no reasonable reader would take them seriously but she recovered damages.

In 1985, the Tory MP Jonathan Aitken was sued for libel by Mrs Pinder-White over an article he wrote that had been published by the *East Kent*

Critic. Mrs Pinder-White was a prominent local Tory, and in his article, Jonathan Aitken had described her and her husband as being similar to JR and Sue Ellen from the TV series *Dallas*. Mrs Pinder-White complained that people understood the article to mean that she was therefore an alcoholic prostitute. The defence was that the words were fair comment and jesting words which were not meant to be taken seriously. The defence of fair comment succeeded.

In another case Mr Matthew Freud, son of the writer and broadcaster Mr Clement Freud, sent out a Christmas card which contained a quip 'Which of our clients did not pay their bill this year (A) Emma Freud, (B) Andrew Wodsworth, (C) Frank Bough?'. Mr Wodsworth sued for libel; it appeared that there had been a dispute over a £4,000 bill, but Mr Wodsworth had sent a cheque for £1,000. The defendant tried to contend that the action was pure humbug, since the bill had not been paid in full, but the jury awarded Mr Wodsworth £10,000 damages.

In 1988, two Dublin lawyers successfully sued an Irish newspaper for an article which claimed that they had come to blows in a cake shop over who should have the last chocolate eclair. The newspaper did not attempt to justify the story but claimed that it was humorous. Not so humorous for the newspaper was the award of £50,000 to each lawyer.

A robust and apparently effective 'defence' was used by the satirical magazine *Private Eye* in *Arkell v Pressdram* (1991), unreported. In that case Mr Arkell's solicitors' letter required an apology and costs and stated of their client: 'His attitude to damages will be governed by the nature of your reply'. The magazine responded:

> We note that Mr Arkell's attitude to damages will be governed by the nature of our reply and would therefore be grateful if you could inform us what his attitude to damages would be were he to learn that the nature of our reply is as follows: 'f*** off'.

A complaint by the columnist Taki Theodoracopulos made in March 1996, about a spoof of his Atticus column in the *Sunday Times*, published by *Private Eye* in April 1995, led to *Private Eye* stating that their response to Taki Theodoracopulos's claim 'is identical to that in the celebrated case of *Arkell v Pressdram* in 1991'. This is not a practice to be recommended, however.

Public figure

There is, as yet, no public figure defence in the UK despite intense lobbying that the Defamation Act 1996 should include such a defence. It is, however, possible that such a defence may be developed judicially and follow the principle established in *New York Times v Sullivan* (1964)

376 US 254. In that case a State Commissioner, Sullivan, sued the *New York Times* over publication of an advertisement criticising the police. The plaintiff's name did not appear in the article, but he successfully claimed that he was identifiable as he was responsible in his state for supervision of the police. However, on appeal it was held that the state could not award damages to a public figure for a false and defamatory statement concerning his official conduct, unless actual malice on the part of the defendant could be proved.

Example

The most recent attempt to use the public figure defence was in *Bennett v Guardian Newspaper* (1995) *The Times*, 28 December when four police officers, who had sued the *Guardian* newspaper for libel, sought to have struck out of the newspaper's defence the *Guardian*'s claim that it was in the public interest to indict a person's character if he was a public figure. The defence of qualified privilege remained but the public figure defence was struck out.

Statutory defence

There may be occasions when statutory protection may be provided, such as under s 1 of the Defamation Act 1996.

Example

In 1995, the controversial appointment of the chairman of Cornwall Health Care Trust led to a libel action (*Kirby-Harris v Baxter* [1995] EMLR 516). After seven months in the position, Mrs Abigail Kirby-Harris resigned after five non-executive directors read her a statement expressing no confidence in her chairmanship. The statement was subsequently sent to five Cornish MPs and released to the press and she immediately instituted libel proceedings. The five non-executive directors of the trust sought to rely on the statutory immunity under s 265 of the Public Health Act 1875, and claimed that the statement was made *bona fide* for the purposes of executing their duties under the National Health Services Act 1977 and the National Health Service and Community Care Act 1990. However, it was held on a preliminary issue that this was a matter of fact for the jury to decide; the case was later settled.

Apology

If a defamatory statement has been published for which a defence is not available, then it may be appropriate for a defendant to publish an immediate correction and apology. Obviously, it should, if possible, be published as part of an agreed settlement but there may be occasions where the plaintiff is intent on pursuing the matter and it will be necessary for the defendant to publish an apology unilaterally as quickly as possible. Reference has already been made to the importance of the positioning of an apology. If it is to be relied on in mitigation, any apology must bear some relation to the position of the original article. For example if the article is a front-page story with a large heading, a small apology in small type at the bottom of one of the inner pages in a newspaper is unlikely to be effective in mitigating the alleged libel.

Example

In 1996 the *Western Daily Press* had published defamatory allegations about the Liberal Democrat leader, Paddy Ashdown, quoting a local activist in his constituency. The allegations were of a very serious nature and he immediately instituted libel proceedings and within one day he had won an unreserved front-page apology and undisclosed damages.

Payment into court

The purpose of a payment into court is to protect the defendant's costs from the date of payment in and to put pressure on the plaintiff to settle. The payment into court, which can be made at any stage of the proceedings and up to and during the trial, is not made known to the judge or jury and a plaintiff will normally have 21 days within which to accept it. If it is accepted, that is an end to the proceedings and the plaintiff is entitled to his taxed costs up to the date of payment in.

If the payment in is not accepted and the matter proceeds to trial, where the plaintiff recovers the same amount of the payment in or less, then he cannot normally recover his costs from the date of payment in. This is on the basis that the plaintiff could have taken the money out of court and settled the action at that earlier date (see also Section IV, Chapter 10). If the plaintiff accepts the payment in, he is also entitled to a statement in open court if the payment in is sufficiently large having regard to the nature of the libel, although the statement will be unilateral, namely the defendant does not have to join in. A payment into court at the appropriate time can therefore be an important weapon for a defendant, where costs (especially the costs of the trial itself) can form such a significant part of any libel action. The cost of a two-week trial with two leading libel silks can amount to £500,000, a significant sum even for a corporate party to proceedings.

Example

In the libel action brought by actor Bill Roache from the *Coronation Street* television series against the *Sun* newspaper in 1992 (see Chapter 1), he claimed that the statement that he was boring, boastful and disliked by his fellow actors was defamatory of him. In that case, he was awarded £50,000 damages. Immediately after the jury's decision, it was disclosed that this was precisely the sum which had been paid into court. The trial judge considered that the plaintiff had had to pursue the matter through to judgment to obtain a permanent injunction, and in his discretion awarded the plaintiff the costs of the trial. The newspaper successfully appealed, and it was held that the only reason the plaintiff went ahead to trial was because he wished to win a larger sum from the jury than the defendant had offered and therefore he was ordered to pay the defendant's costs from the date of payment in, which of course included the substantial costs of the trial.

Security for costs

As in all litigation, it is open to a defendant to apply for a foreign plaintiff or a corporate plaintiff, which may be trading while insolvent, to give security for costs. The reasoning behind this is that should the defendant be successful there should be some guarantee that any costs order against the plaintiff can be satisfied. A plaintiff who is resident abroad may not have assets in this country; a company which is trading while insolvent may not have funds available to satisfy a judgment.

Examples

In *Condliffe v Hislop* (1995) *The Times*, 3 November an attempt was made by *Private Eye* to obtain an order that an impecunious plaintiff, not resident outside the jurisdiction, should lodge security for costs. The facts were that, after the plaintiff instituted proceedings for libel against the defendant, he and his wife were adjudicated bankrupt. The plaintiff's mother then gave an undertaking to pay any court order in respect of the defendant's costs but the undertaking was subsequently withdrawn. The defendant sought to claim that the mother was a woman of modest means. However, the court held that as the crime of maintenance, namely supporting another person's litigation, had been abolished, a close relative could be regarded as lawfully justified in giving financial assistance and the order for security was not made.

A slightly different point arose in *Chequepoint SARL v McClelland* (1996) *The Times*, 18 June. In that case, a foreign company, ordinarily resident in a member state of the European Union, was ordered to give security for costs. On appeal it was held that in making that order, the court had not exercised its discretion in a discriminatory manner contrary to the principles of Community law, since it had treated such a company no differently from an English registered company which might also be required to give security under s 726 of the Companies Act 1985.

Check list

(1) In relation to defences of release and satisfaction what evidence is there to satisfy a court that all the parties had agreed to the settlement?

(2) Was there an apology offered; was it a brief apology? Were amendments by the plaintiff considered? How quickly was it offered?

(3) Did the plaintiff consent to publication? Is there evidence of that consent?

(4) In relation to statutory limitation, when did the plaintiff first hear of the alleged libel?

(5) In relation to innocent dissemination, how did the plaintiff first learn of the alleged libel? By notification directly from the plaintiff or by a newspaper report of an injunction?

(6) Does the defendant come within one of the exceptions similar to or analogous to those set out in s 1(3) of the Defamation Act 1996 as not being primarily responsible for publication?

(7) Has the defendant taken all reasonable care?

(8) Did the defendant do anything which contributed to publication of the alleged libel? How responsible is the defendant for the publication? Was the publication such that the defendant could have been aware that it was likely to contain a defamatory statement?

(9) In relation to general bad reputation are there any facts that can be adduced to be added to the defence?

(10) Should a payment into court be made?

(11) Should without prejudice negotiations be initiated with a view to an amicable settlement?

(12) Is the plaintiff a foreign resident against whom an application for security for costs can be made?

Related Actions and Relief Available to Plaintiffs

In this Section, an examination will be made of actions related to libel and the remedies available to a successful plaintiff.

Chapter 8

Related Actions

Criminal libel

Definition

A prosecution for criminal libel may be brought where the libel is so serious that a civil remedy may be deemed inadequate, for example, where the libel is so grave that breach of peace is imminent, namely that the words may provoke public disorder. However, such instances are rare.

Application

Although criminal libel has not been abolished, it would seem that certain of the situations where prosecution for criminal libel might be appropriate will now be covered by other legislation such as, for example, the Race Relations Act 1976 and the Public Order Act 1986. There are four important differences between criminal libel and a civil action for libel:

(1) If the defence seeks to show that the words are true then in addition the defence must show that the words were published for the public benefit; therefore, even if the defamatory statements can be proved to be true, that may not necessarily be a sufficient defence.

(2) There is no requirement, as in civil libel, for publication to a third person. If the libel is sufficiently serious, even if it is only published to the plaintiff, prosecution for criminal libel can succeed.

(3) It is possible for a representative of a deceased person to bring a prosecution for criminal libel since if a serious defamatory statement is made about a deceased person, with the intention of injuring surviving members of the family, that can constitute criminal libel.

(4) A prosecution for criminal libel cannot be brought against a news-

paper without leave from the judge. A private prosecution can be commenced by either an application to a magistrate or to a High Court judge but in the case of a newspaper there must be an order from the judge in chambers.

Examples

An early example was the case where the founder of *The Times*, John Walter, accused the Royal Dukes of hypocrisy in 1789 when they gave thanks for the recovery of King George from madness. For his pains he was fined £50.00 and imprisoned in Newgate.

In recent years there have been very few prosecutions for criminal libel. Sir James Goldsmith obtained leave to prosecute the then editor of *Private Eye*, Richard Ingrams, for criminal libel in 1977 but the prosecution was later dropped. *Private Eye* had made certain allegations against Mr James Goldsmith as he then was. These concerned his alleged involvement in a conspiracy following the disappearance of Lord Lucan, widely suspected to be responsible for the murder of his children's nanny. In addition to the proceedings for criminal libel brought against the editor of *Private Eye*, Sir James Goldsmith also issued 84 writs in civil libel proceedings (see Section II, Chapter 7).

In deciding whether to grant leave for a prosecution in respect of an article in a newspaper, the judge is entitled to consider whether or not the newspaper will have a substantive defence.

Example

In *Desmond v Thorne* [1982] 3 All ER 268 an application for leave to bring a prosecution for criminal libel against the *Sunday People* over an article which had described the complainant as a violent and drunken bully was refused because of evidence obtained by the newspaper which appeared to support the statement.

Defences

Truth and public benefit

The main defence is provided under s 6 of the Libel Act 1843 which provides that it is a defence to an action for criminal libel to prove that the words were true *and* that they were published for the public benefit. In addition s 5 of the Defamation Act 1952 (see Section II, Chapter 3) does not apply to proceedings for criminal libel and the defendant must therefore prove the truth of each and every statement.

Privilege

The defence of absolute privilege can also be applied under s 4 of the

Law of Libel Amendment Act 1888 which provides for a defence of absolute privilege if it is a fair and accurate report provided the publication was not blasphemous or published maliciously. Qualified privilege also applies as in civil law.

If the proprietor of a newspaper was unaware that it contained a criminal libel, that can operate as a defence under s 7 of the Libel Act 1843.

Penalties

Section 4 of the Libel Act 1843 provides that anybody who maliciously publishes a defamatory libel, knowing it to be false, shall be liable to imprisonment for a term not exceeding two years and subject to a fine. If the defendant did not know the libel was false, then imprisonment will be for a maximum of only one year (s 5).

Section 6 expressly provides that the penalty provided for in ss 4 and 5 may be aggravated if the plea of justification is persisted in but unsuccessful.

As mentioned above, some of the situations where a prosecution for criminal libel might have been appropriate have now been pre-empted by the race relations legislation. In addition, there are provisions under the Post Office Act 1953 and the Malicious Communications Act 1988 providing for prosecution of threatening, abusive or insulting communications whether poison pen letters or otherwise.

Example

The book *The Satanic Verses*, by the prize winning author Salman Rushdie, contained some derogatory remarks about the Prophet Mohammed. As a result of an orchestrated campaign, both in the Asian community in the UK and later in India and Pakistan, the Ayatollah Khomeini of Iran issued a *fatwa* on 14 February 1989 urging all Moslems to kill Salman Rushdie. The author has consequently had to live in hiding for a number of years, protected round the clock by Special Branch officers. Several years after the *fatwa*, a Pakistan film company prepared a film entitled *International Guerillas*. In it Salman Rushdie was portrayed as a sadistic terrorist. Speculation that criminal libel proceedings should be brought against the company was silenced when Mr Salman Rushdie stated that he was totally opposed to any such prosecution and indeed would testify for the defence.

Blasphemy

Definition

The criminal offence of blasphemy is committed when material is published which outrages and insults the Christian religion with comments about God, Jesus, holy personages, or articles of faith. It is immaterial whether the words are spoken or written and the intention of the publisher is irrelevant.

The Christian religion includes all branches of Roman Catholicism, Methodist and Baptist but not any other religion.

Examples

Whitehouse v Lemon (1978) 67 Cr App Rep 70 is one of the most controversial blasphemy cases of recent times. The case arose out of a poem published in 1976 by *Gay News*, a magazine for homosexual men. The poem appeared to imply that Jesus Christ was homosexual and when the authorities refused to take any action, Mrs Mary Whitehouse of the National Viewers and Listeners Association, obtained permission from a judge for a private prosecution. The prosecution was able to establish that *Gay News* and its editor were responsible for publication and that persons who had read it had been shocked and angered by it as it was clearly an attack on Christianity. By a majority verdict, *Gay News* and its editor were guilty of publishing a blasphemous libel, a verdict upheld both on appeal and to the House of Lords.

While the arguments on behalf of *Gay News* that the prosecution had to show both intent and a likelihood that a breach of the peace were advanced, these were rejected by the Law Lords and the trial judges referred to a useful definition of blasphemy as 'any contemptuous, reviling, scurrilous or ludicrous matter relating to God, Jesus Christ or the Bible or the formulaic of the Church of England'. A distinction was drawn between publishing critical comment about the Christian religion as opposed to scurrilous and intemperate attacks. Although the furore caused by the case led to many calls for the abolition of blasphemy or its extension to all religions, no amendments to the law were made. Indeed, it was invoked again in 1989 when a video entitled *Visions of Ecstasy* about Saint Teresa of Avila which portrayed her as handling Jesus Christ's dead body in a sexual way, was banned on the grounds that the video was blasphemous.

As has been seen the novel *The Satanic Verses* by Salman Rushdie contained on a small number of pages unsympathetic portrayals of Mohammed the Prophet including describing him as involved in sexual peccadilloes. Several attempts were made in the UK by various groups to have Salman Rushdie and the publishers prosecuted for blasphemy but it was held that blasphemy related only to the Christian religion and therefore it was not applicable to derogatory comments about the Prophet Mohammed.

The same defence available to a proprietor unaware of the blasphemous publication, is applicable as with criminal libel (see under 'Defences' above).

Malicious falsehood

Definition

Where words have been published which may not be defamatory but which can be proved to:

(a) be false;

(b) have been published maliciously; and

(c) have caused special or actual damage;

then the plaintiff has a remedy for an action for damages for malicious falsehood. The malice, which must be established by the plaintiff, can be shown either in that the defendant knew that the words were false when he published them, or that he knew the words were likely to injure and was recklessly indifferent as to whether they were true or false. Carelessness or negligence is not sufficient.

In contrast to libel, legal aid is available for malicious falsehood. Moreover, unlike libel, the plaintiff has the burden of proving falsity and malice in order to succeed, as well as damage.

The claim under malicious falsehood may also be formulated under slander of title or slander of goods, see below.

Examples

In *Joyce v Sengupta and Today* [1993] 1 WLR 337 a former ladies maid to Princess Anne was accused in the *Today* newspaper of having stolen and sold private letters belonging to the Princess. As a result the maid lost her job and had difficulty in finding employment. As she was unable to afford proceedings for libel, she obtained legal aid and sued the newspaper for malicious falsehood. The Court of Appeal held that she was entitled to bring a claim of malicious falsehood even though a claim of libel may have been more appropriate. She was able to show that the statements made about her were false, that the newspaper had been malicious and that the falsehood had thereby caused her damage. She was awarded £25,000 damages.

An unusual extension to malicious falsehood arose in *Kaye v Sunday Sport* (1990), unreported. In that case a television actor, Gordon Kaye, had had a serious accident in the street. Journalists and a photographer from the *Sunday Sport* newspaper infiltrated the actor's room while he was still very ill in hospital and prepared an interview and photographs. An injunction was applied for on behalf of the actor seeking to prevent publication on the grounds of libel, trespass, passing off and malicious falsehood. It was held that it would be a malicious falsehood to publish anything which implied that the actor had consented to publication of the photographs or the interview when he was clearly too ill to have given such consent, that once they were aware of the plaintiff's objection, publication would be malicious and that the actor would suffer damage since the value of the story which he wished to sell himself would be diminished. This decision was upheld on appeal.

In 1996 MP Rupert Allason sued the *Daily Mirror* for malicious falsehood over a 'campaign of spite' which he claimed the newspaper had waged against him. The claim arose out of a story which claimed that 50 MPs had challenged the plaintiff to demonstrate his concern for Maxwell pensioners by giving them the estimated £250,000 libel damages he had won earlier from the *Mirror* newspaper. The facts were that the Commons early day motion had seven signatories, had only 31 names on it when it 'died' and the amount of damages recovered was £200,000. The judge found firstly that the story had been false; secondly that it had been published by the Mirror Group with malice, although the two journalists sued had not been seriously involved or acted maliciously; thirdly that any claim arising out of the publication had been corrected by publication of a correction and apology. The plaintiff, however, had failed to show that he had suffered any financial damage and lost his case.

In 1996, a claim for malicious falsehood by Vodafone against Orange, a rival mobile phone company, failed (*Vodafone Group plc v Orange Personal Communications Services Ltd* (1996) *The Times*, 31 August). Vodafone had claimed that the advertising slogan by Orange claiming £20 a month savings in comparison with Vodafone and Cellnet was untrue. The judge held that the words would be understood as meaning that Orange users in comparison with Vodafone users would have had to pay an average of £20 less per month for the same usage. He held that it was 'preposterous' for Vodafone to claim that Orange had committed perjury in making this claim in its advertisements.

Under s 5 of the Defamation Act 1996, the limitation period for actions for malicious falsehood is reduced from three years to one year.

Slander of title

Definition

An action may be brought for slander of title where false words are spoken or written about a person's title, the statement is made maliciously and pecuniary damage has been caused. The plaintiff has to show that:

(a) the false statement about his title or his goods has been made to a third person; and

(b) the statement was made maliciously and that as a result of which he has suffered loss.

Under s 3 of the Defamation Act 1952, loss does not have to be proved if the words are either calculated to cause pecuniary damage and are published in writing and other permanent form, or that they are calculated to cause pecuniary damage in respect of any profession, office or trade held by the plaintiff at the time of publication.

Examples

In *Sparter-Florida Music Group v Kruger* (1988), there was a dispute between the plaintiffs and one of the defendants who had engaged them as music publishers from 1970. In 1970, they wound up their joint company, whose business was transferred to the first plaintiff company. The plaintiffs claimed the defendant, Kruger, had purported to licence reproduction of 158 songs in which the plaintiffs owned copyright and had collected substantial royalties. The claim was, *inter alia*, infringement of copyright and slander of the plaintiff's title to copyright. On an interlocutory application, it was held that since the alleged infringement was outside the UK, the Copyright Act 1956 only created actionable wrongs in respect of acts done within the UK and in the absence of any evidence of threats by the defendants to make claim to other songs, no injunction would lie in respect of slander of title to the first 71 songs.

In *Micro Data Information Services Ltd v Rivendale and Cryne* [1991] FSR 681, where there was a dispute between two software houses, it was held that the action was not slander of title or defamation but interference with contract.

Where the statement alleged to be slander of title is made, for example, by a solicitor or agent on instructions from a client, a defence of privilege will attach to that solicitor or agent.

Slander of goods

Definition

An action for slander of goods will lie where a false statement disparages the goods of a plaintiff as opposed to the plaintiff himself. The statement must be proved to be false and must be distinguished from 'mere trade puff'. The statement must be proved to be published maliciously and unless it comes within the provision of s 3 of the Defamation Act 1952 referred to above, special damage must be proved. As in slander of title the onus is on the plaintiff to prove that the words are false and details must be given of pecuniary damage suffered.

Examples

In the leading case of *White v Melin* [1895] AC 154, the defendant, who sold food manufactured by the plaintiff, affixed a label to the plaintiff's food claiming that it was more nutritious than the plaintiff's medicine. This was held to be mere 'trade puff'. This is to be distinguished from instances where the disparaging statement is put in a scientific form; for example, an allegation that mineral water contained damaging bacteria, which a reasonable reader would be inclined to take seriously.

McDonald v Steel and Morris (above) is an action for libel since it is alleged to defame the company responsible rather than the product.

It is interesting that in America there is now a provision that a person can be sued if they make 'a false disparagement of perishable goods products'. This development has been as a result of pressure by America's vegetable and fruit growers and the powerful chemical industry in response to growing public concern about pesticides, chemicals and sprays used to keep fruit and vegetables fresh.

False attribution of authorship

Definition

False attribution of authorship is the appropriate cause of action where a person's name has been wrongly affixed to words which are not his. For example, if a writer is commissioned to write a piece for a newspaper, but when the article is published with the writer's name, the words are entirely different and written in such a fashion as to be defamatory of the plaintiff in addition to any claim for libel, the plaintiff may also be able to sue for false attribution of authorship under s 84 of the Copyright, Designs and Patents Act 1988. This provides a remedy where authorship is falsely attributed to the plaintiff and copies are issued to the public. Damages will normally amount to a licence fee or the usual sum of money paid for the plaintiff's work.

False attribution is not a widely used cause of action and is normally seen as an addition to a claim for infringement of copyright.

Example

In *Moore v News of the World* (see above) in addition to the award of £4,300 for libel, Dorothy Squires was awarded £100 for false attribution because the headline: 'How my Love for the Saint went Sour by Dorothy

Squires' was untrue because she had not written the article. In the later case of *Noah v Shuba* [1991] FCR 140 (before a judge alone), the award was £7,250 for libel and £250 for false attribution. In that case, the plaintiff, who was a consultant epidemiologist, had written a book *A Guide to Hygienic Skin Piercing*. The first defendant was the Managing Director of the company which employed the second defendant. The company sold products for use by beauty therapists. The plaintiff supplied a copy of a general part of his book to the first defendant. There was subsequently a meeting between the two men and later, after Mr Shuba had delivered a lecture based on extracts from Mr Noah's book, an article was prepared for publication in the magazine *Health and Beauty Salon*. The article covered work from the plaintiff's book but also included a sentence with which the plaintiff was not in agreement and which did not represent his view on the clinical points. He sued for libel and false attribution and was awarded £7,250 in respect of libel and £250 for false attribution of authorship.

Check list

Criminal libel

(1) Is the libel very serious?

(2) Has the publication of the libel been likely to provoke a breach of the peace, even if it is true?

(3) If it relates to a person who is dead, is it made with intention to injure surviving members of the family?

(4) Would civil damages be an adequate remedy?

Blasphemy

(1) Is it an outrageous comment on the Christian religion or any aspects of it?

(2) Does it go beyond general critical comment?

Malicious falsehood

(1) Can it be shown that the statement is false?

(2) How can it be shown that the maker of the statement was malicious?

(3) What is the damage that can be proved to have been suffered by the plaintiff?

Slander of title

(1) Is the statement false?
(2) Has it been made maliciously?
(3) Is there actual evidence of pecuniary damage?

Slander of goods

(1) Is the statement false?
(2) Can it be shown to have been made maliciously?
(3) Is it mere trade puff?
(4) Is there evidence of actual pecuniary damage?

False attribution of authorship

(1) Has the plaintiff's name been wrongly affixed to matter he did not write?
(2) Has this been published?
(3) Has it caused, or is it likely to cause, damage to the plaintiff?

Chapter 9

Relief for Plaintiffs

Relief available

The relief which can be available to a plaintiff in a libel action includes:
    (a) damages;
    (b) an injunction to prevent repetition of the libel; and
    (c) a statement in open court clearing his name.
The main remedies sought in a libel action are normally damages and an injunction. The award of costs is at the judge's discretion.

Damages

Damages fall into five categories namely, general, special, exemplary or punitive, aggravated, contemptuous or nominal.

General

General compensatory damages are designed:
    (a) to compensate for damage to reputation;
    (b) to compensate for hurt feelings; and
    (c) to vindicate the plaintiff for bringing the action.
Damage in a libel action and certain slander actions is presumed, so that the plaintiff does not have to prove that he has suffered as a result of the alleged libel, although he can if he wishes call evidence to show that he has been ostracised by his friends or otherwise harmed. The assessment of the general damages is at present by the jury, which will normally hear libel actions, unless it is one of the rare cases not to have a jury. Occasionally an action is likely to be of such length and complexity that a judge will hear the matter alone. This happened in *Upjohn v BBC* (see Section II, Chapter 3). The case arose out of allegations broadcast by the BBC that the drug Halcion, manufactured by the Upjohn company, had unforeseen side effects. Because the action was concerned

with scientific evidence, it was heard by a judge alone. In the current longest running libel case in the UK namely, *McDonalds v Steel and Morris,* because of the number of allegations and the complexity of the evidence, this libel action is also being heard by a judge alone.

In assessing general damages juries commonly were given no explicit guidance, yet for the majority of jurors on major libel cases, which tend to be reported, it is the first occasion on which they have been involved in any way with libel and not surprisingly awards can vary considerably, as is shown in appendices A and D.

Examples

The highest award made by a jury was in November 1989 when Lord Aldington was awarded £1.5 damages for a libel implicating him in the forceable repatriation at the end of the Second World War of prisoners-of-war. Although a jury will normally consider, as well as the reputation of the plaintiff and the nature of the libel, the extent of the publication and whether there was any apology offered, it is interesting to note that the Aldington record award of damages was in respect of a pamphlet of which 10,000 copies were distributed.

This contrasts with the case of actor Jason Connery, who in 1992 sued the *Sun* for a statement that he had refused to fight in the Gulf War which implied that he was a coward. Although the *Sun* has a circulation of over four million, he received only £35,000 damages.

In the case of Teresa Gorman who sued her constituency chairman for libel over a pamphlet circulated by him purporting to come from her, only 93 copies were circulated but she recovered, at first instance, damages of £150,000 (subsequently reduced on appeal to £50,000).

Although it is not possible to know how juries arrive at their decision, it must be presumed that the conduct of the two parties to the proceedings is a factor taken into account. Where, for example, the defendants have persisted in a defamatory allegation and only offered an apology shortly before the trial, this is presumed to affect a jury's assessment of damages. Similarly, where a plaintiff has perhaps behaved in an obstinate manner, rejecting letters of apology, this may also be reflected in the jury's verdict.

Example

A somewhat perverse verdict was given by the jury in the case where English cricketers, Ian Botham and Allan Lamb sued the Pakistan cricketer, Imran Khan, for libel in 1996. Botham and Lamb claimed that Imran Khan had accused them of cheating and of being lower class. Imran Khan denied the allegations, attempted justification, although this was withdrawn during the trial, and he also offered to apologise.The 14-day trial enthralled both cricketing fans and the general public, particularly with the number of cricketing metaphors employed by both leading counsel and the judge throughout. The jury found in favour of the defendant, Imran Khan, leaving Botham and Lamb with a substantial bill of costs. After the verdict it was reported that Botham and Lamb were appealing and seeking a retrial.

While the practice is that juries can be given no specific guidance, there have been attempts in recent years to give the jury parameters in which to consider damages such as 'the price of a family car or terraced house' but juries have been surprisingly inconsistent. The libel barrister, George Carman QC, recently proposed that juries should be given guidance in four levels of damages to avoid the telephone number awards which he has described as 'irrational and extreme'. The four categories were: trivial, moderate, serious and grave, each carrying a specific damages award range, say £1,000–£15,000 for trivial libel. While preserving the jury system, it would have provided a scale not dissimilar to personal injury damages, with which libel damages are often adversely compared.

However, since then, in a landmark decision in 1995, in hearing an appeal by the *Sunday Mirror* newspaper against an award to Elton John of £350,000 damages (*Elton John v MGN* [1996] 2 All ER 35), the Court of Appeal laid down definitive guidelines to be given to juries to assist them in assessing damages. For the first time these make specific reference to the comparison with personal injury awards.

Guidelines

In the *Elton John* case (see Section V, Chapter 11), Elton John had sued the *Sunday Mirror* newspaper over an article which stated that he was suffering from an eating disorder and had been seen to regurgitate food at a Hollywood party. He had successfully alleged that the article meant that he was a liar and a hypocrite in claiming that he had recovered from his eating disorder. He was awarded £275,000 exemplary damages, because evidence was given that he was never at the party and compensatory damages of £75,000.

In hearing the appeal in December 1995, the court reduced the award of compensatory damages from £75,000 to £25,000 and reduced the exemplary damages from £275,000 to £50,000. The appeal, which was under s 8 of the Courts and Legal Services Act 1980 (see Section V, Chapter 11) gave the Court of Appeal the opportunity to consider the question of damages in great detail. The judgment of the Court of Appeal, which was both clear and comprehensive, considered three areas in coming to its recommended guidelines:

(1) Whether juries should be reminded of previous libel awards. They concluded that this might be unreliable.

(2) Whether reference could be made to awards approved or substituted by the Court of Appeal. The court felt that as and when such a framework was established, such reference could be useful, and indeed there are a few reported Court of Appeal decisions.

(3) Whether a correlation could be made with personal injury awards. It was felt that a jury could be informed of the maximum conventional award for pain and suffering and loss of amenity to a plaintiff suffering from severe brain damage, which would amount to £125,000 and the juries could be asked to consider whether the injury to reputation of which the plaintiff complains 'should fairly justify any greater compensation'. Juries could also be referred to any number of personal injuries awards if it was felt appropriate, not just the maximum. It could also be appropriate for juries to be given an approximate range of figures.

It remains to be seen how well the guidelines will be applied in practice. In a case only days after the Elton John guidelines were given MP Peter Bottomley who sued the *Sunday Express* was awarded £40,000 damages. The award was clearly influenced by those guidelines. However, only six weeks later, in February 1996, a Dr Percy sued Mirror Group Newspapers over three articles which implied that he had contributed to the death of a patient who was forced to fly 200 miles for treatment. The award in that case was £625,000 damages and the guidelines were not applied. The matter was later settled before appeal for damages of £125,000.

Special

Where a plaintiff can show, for example, that he had as a result of the libel been forced to leave his employment, the loss of earnings can be claimed as special damages. Where special damages are claimed, particulars of the claim must be set out in the statement of claim. Similarly, if a plaintiff company can show that its share price has been affected by the alleged libel, or has lost specific business or a general downturn in profits, that could form the basis of a claim for special damages.

Example

In 1993 Gordon and Anita Roddick, Directors of the Body Shop, and The Body Shop company itself, the well known retail chain, sued Channel 4 for damages. Channel 4 had broadcast a documentary which cast doubt on the integrity of certain of the claims of the Body Shop in relation to animal testing. A substantial claim for special damages was made and after the trial the three plaintiffs were awarded £1,000 general damages each for libel and the company was awarded special damages of £273,000.

Aggravated

Aggravated damages are awarded for any increased or additional hurt caused to the plaintiff's feelings by the defendant's conduct. If the defendant, for example, repeats the libel after the writ or persists in his claims in open court *via* a plea of justification, and if the defence is unsuccessful, or the defendant fails to apologise, aggravated damages can be awarded. Such damages should be specifically claimed in the statement of claim (see Section IV, Chapter 10).

Example

In 1995, the football manager, Graeme Souness, sued Mirror Group Newspapers over an article about the break-up of his marriage entitled 'You Dirty Rat'. He was awarded £750,000 damages (later reduced by consent shortly before appeal to £100,000), a figure which must inevitably have been increased by the defendants' conduct, which included a plea of justification.

Exemplary or punitive

If the defendant suspected that the words were false and had made a calculated assessment that any damages awarded against him were likely to be outweighed by the profit to him from publishing the alleged libel, then if the plaintiff can establish this fact, this can give rise to an award of exemplary damages. Such claims are not common and must be specifically pleaded in the statement of claim (see Section IV, Chapter 10).

Examples

The leading case is *Cassell & Company Ltd v Broome* [1972] AC 1027. In that case a Captain Broome RN had sued for libel over a book *PQ17* containing serious allegations about his conduct in relation to escorting a convoy in the Second World War. Evidence was given in the trial that the publisher, although notified of the alleged libel before publication, had decided to continue with publishing the book and the plaintiff was awarded exemplary damages of £40,000, which were upheld on appeal.

Punitive damages were also awarded in the case brought in 1993 by the pop star Elton John against the *Sunday Mirror* (see under 'General' above). A case brought by the late Robert Maxwell against *Private Eye* in 1986 also resulted in an award of punitive damages. *Private Eye* had alleged that the late Robert Maxwell had financed a trip abroad for Neil Kinnock in the hope of ennoblement. In fact, he had twice rejected a peerage and he was awarded £5,000 in respect of the article, together with £50,000 for exemplary damages. No doubt the jury, in considering that award, took into account the remark in the witness box of the then editor Richard Ingrams, when he said under oath that the apologies in *Private Eye* were the only deliberate lies the magazine had ever published.

Lord Linley in 1990 took the unusual step for the Royal Family, of suing the *Today* newspaper for libel over a story that he had been banned from a particular public house; he was awarded £35,000 damages, of which £30,000 was expressed to be exemplary. Despite evidence of three journalists, the jury apparently accepted that the story had been made up. The newspaper announced that it was going to appeal and subsequently, Lord Linley waived the punitive element of the damages.

Contemptuous or nominal

These are awarded for libel where the jury, while finding that the words were defamatory and that the defendant has no defence, does not feel that the reputation of the plaintiff has been damaged by the libel.

Examples

In 1994 a Mr Wraith sued his ex-wife for slander alleging that she had been damaging his reputation by claiming that he had frequented brothels. The ex-wife pleaded justification and the jury awarded £69 damages, being the price of a bottle of champagne at a brothel allegedly visited by the plaintiff. In 1960 a Dr Dering sued Leon Uris, the author of the book *Exodus,* over an allegation that he had operated on concentration camp victims without an anaesthetic. He recovered a halfpenny damages.

In 1995 a Dr Chohan sued Oxford University Press over allegations in a book about the history of Sikhs. He claimed that the book portrayed him as corrupt and included allegations that he had been involved in a plot to assassinate Mrs Ghandi. The defendants pleaded justification and included in its defence video taped news items showing Dr Chohan commenting on the assassination of Mrs Ghandi. The jury agreed that he had been libelled but clearly they felt his reputation had not been harmed and awarded 1p damages, no doubt taking into account the steps taken by the defendant to reduce the damages in removing offending copies from bookshops.

Injunctions

There are three categories of injunctions: *quia timet*, interlocutory and permanent. *Quia timet* is an injunction to restrain anticipated publication; an interlocutory injunction is to restrain publication pending the trial of the action and a permanent injunction is to restrain publication after the parties have agreed terms or there has been a decision in the plaintiff's favour. The basis for which injunctions can be granted in defamation actions are an exception to the general rule laid down in *American Cyanamid Co v Ethicon Ltd* [1975] AC 396 because of the importance of free speech. This means that where the defendant shows the court that he intends to plead justification or privilege an injunction is unlikely to be granted.

Quia timet and interlocutory injunctions are frequently applied for *ex parte* and, as with any *ex parte* application for an injunction, if it is granted, it is usually on terms that the parties return on notice within two to three days. As with any equitable remedy, a plaintiff must come to equity 'with clean hands' and so full disclosure on an *ex parte* application is essential. The plaintiff must, of course, show that the words are obviously defamatory and must act with all speed when seeking interlocutory relief.

Examples

The late Robert Maxwell was never able to obtain an injunction to prevent publication of Tom Bower's biography of him, *The Outsider*, because he did not have 'clean hands'. However, Maxwell succeeded in his objective of preventing distribution of the book by immediately notifying all booksellers that the book contained an alleged libel in respect of which he had issued proceedings so that they had no defence of innocent dissemination and could have been sued for libel in the same way as the publishers (see Section II, Chapter 7). This is a clear example of the use of the so-called 'gagging writ'.

In *The Church of Scientology v Penguin Books Ltd* (1986), unreported, 22 October, CA, the plaintiff, the Church of Scientology, sought an injunction against the defendant publishers and the author, Russell Miller, to prevent the publication of a book entitled *The Bare-Faced Messiah* about the founder of the Church of Scientology, L Ron Hubbard. The application for the injunction was refused because evidence was given that the plaintiff had been aware that the book was being written over a year before the application was made. Also the application was made only a week before publication and evidence was given that the plaintiff had obtained a proof copy of the book approximately eight weeks before. The injunction was refused because the plaintiff had not acted quickly enough.

Quia timet

Quia timet injunctions are sought to prevent the proposed publication of an alleged libel. It is essential if such an application is to succeed that the plaintiff should have the clearest possible evidence of the defamatory words that are to be published. A belief that the defendant is likely to publish defamatory words will not normally be sufficient.

Example

British Data Management plc v Boxer Commercials Removal plc (1996) *The Times*, 28 February, CA. In that case, an injunction was sought to restrain publication of statements to the effect that a company was guilty of civil wrongs or criminal offences in relation to the contents of its accounts and annual reports. The actual word or words of the threatened publication were not pleaded and it was held that a *quia timet* injunction failed. In a similar case, an application for an injunction against a newspaper failed because the plaintiff could only produce a list of questions which had been faxed from a reporter of the newspaper, together with the reporter's notes of the conversation, and this was held to be insufficient to show precisely what the newspaper was planning to publish. A draft of the article that the defendant's newspaper proposes to publish should normally be exhibited to an affidavit supporting an *ex parte* application for a *quia timet* injunction.

Interlocutory

After publication it is open to the plaintiff to apply to the court for an interlocutory injunction restraining further publication. In the case of a newspaper which appears for one day only, this may be academic but in the case of a book it can frequently be very important. An interlocutory injunction will not normally be granted where the defendant shows that he intends to plead justification. However, it can happen that an *ex parte* injunction may be granted and even if the injunction is lifted at the *inter partes* hearing after, say, two days, the results can still be damaging for a defendant publisher.

For example, after the *ex parte* injunction has been obtained, the plaintiff can then notify all booksellers and distributors who stock the publication that an injunction has been obtained because the book contained material which is alleged to be defamatory. Upon receipt of this notification, booksellers and distributors can no longer claim to be 'innocent disseminators' and therefore could be sued for libel in exactly the same way as the original publisher. Therefore they may withdraw the publication from sale even if the injunction is subsequently lifted after two days and the defendant gives them notice that the injunction has been lifted. This is because they may consider that until the matter is resolved they will be at risk for selling material which they know is defamatory. Similarly, in the case of a newspaper *ex parte* injunction obtained by a plaintiff, even if it only lasts for 24 hours, it could mean that a topical story may lose its value and publication may be prevented altogether.

Examples

In *Charles St George v Penguin Books Ltd* (1984), unreported, a plaintiff underwriter obtained an *ex parte* injunction against publication of a book entitled *Lloyd's of London*. Although the injunction was lifted two days later, damage was caused to the sales of the book because of the publicity which the injunction received. The booksellers became aware, because of newspaper reports of the injunction, that the book contained defamatory material; thus their defence of innocent dissemination was destroyed and certain bookshops declined to continue selling. The matter was later settled.

In *Harakas v Baltic Mercantile Shipping Exchange Ltd* [1982] 2 All ER 701, the plaintiff applied for an injunction to prevent the posting of a notice in the Baltic Exchange. The defendants were able to show that they had good grounds for posting such a notice and also pleaded that publication, on the board within the Baltic Exchange and only seen by members, was an occasion of qualified privilege. The application for an interlocutory injunction failed.

In *Bestobell v Bigg* [1975] FSR 421, a paint company applied for an interlocutory injunction against Mr Biggs, who had painted his house with Carsons paint manufactured by the plaintiff. After a short period the paint started peeling, and he placed a notice outside the house saying 'these premises have been painted with Carsons paint'. The plaintiff paint manufacturer sought an injunction, but Mr Biggs claimed that he was going to justify and the injunction was not granted.

In contrast was the case of a disgruntled author who had paraded up and down outside his former publishers' office with a placard saying 'Conmen and crooks run ... Books'. In that case an interlocutory injunction was granted.

Permanent

As will be seen (Section IV, Chapter 10), the writ will normally seek a permanent injunction preventing repetition of the libel. In the case of books, newspapers and television, where such an injunction is granted at the end of the trial, care needs to be taken with cuttings, library copies, databases and research material, to ensure that the injunction is complied with and there is no inadvertent republication. Similarly, in any settlement, a term of settlement should always require that the details of the settlement and any apology in a statement in open court should be filed in the cuttings library or database and that the item should not be syndicated. With television, terms should include not only no rebroadcasting, but also no sale or use by third parties.

Examples

A libel action brought by two police officers against Ian Botham in respect of the passage in his autobiography which criticised their questioning of his wife over an incident relating to cannabis, resulted in the book being amended and a permanent injunction being granted (see Section II, Chapter 7). When inadvertently the paperback was released still containing the offending passage, this was clearly a breach of the permanent injunction, and the paperback had to be swiftly withdrawn.

At the end of the action by Lord Aldington against Tolstoy and Watts in 1989, the defendants were ordered to pay Lord Aldington £1.5m for publishing a defamatory leaflet. The trial also imposed a permanent injunction against repetition of the libel by either of the defendants. In 1995, Watts was jailed for 18 months for contempt of court for repeating the libel in breach of the permanent injunction.

In 1992, Kathleen Etchingham, a girlfriend of the late Jimmy Hendrix, sued Monika Danneman, a woman who claimed to be his 'fiancee', for libel. The matter was settled on terms which included a permanent undertaking embodied in a court order not to repeat the libel which had been published in a typescript of Danneman's memoirs of the 1960s. In 1995, however, it came to the attention of Ms Etchingham that the libel had effectively been repeated in a book written by Ms Danneman and an application was made to commit her for contempt of court because she had breached the undertaking given not to repeat the words complained of or any similar libel.

In any negotiated settlement it is advantageous for a plaintiff to insist upon the defendant giving undertakings which are incorporated in a court order. The precise words alleged, publication of which is sought to be prevented by the undertaking, should also be specified with as much particularity as possible. Any breach of those undertakings will therefore be a contempt of court.

Statement in open court

As the purpose of a libel action is to obtain compensation for real or perceived damage to reputation, even if the action is settled, the plaintiff may be entitled to have a statement read in open court vindicating his reputation in public, if he has accepted a payment into court or has insisted upon a statement in court as part of a negotiated settlement. This is not however, a form of relief that can be claimed in the writ. The statement will contain a lengthy section, outlining in as much detail as the plaintiff deems is reasonable, the alleged libel. It will go on to state that the defendant recognises that the article was wholly without foundation and has agreed to apologise and to pay the plaintiff a substantial sum by way of damages and to reimburse him in respect of his costs. On behalf of the defendant a statement is then made agreeing with everything that has been stated.

Finally, on behalf of the plaintiff a statement is made asking that the record be withdrawn and if appropriate an order for payment out of any monies paid into court, but the sum in court is not mentioned.

It is never the practice to reveal an exact amount of any damages in a statement in open court and the word 'substantial' can be used for a range of sums. Frequently, there will be a confidentiality agreement stating that the amount of damages should not be revealed but in the absence of such an agreement, where the matter is of press interest, the sum is very often revealed in discussions with journalists after the reading of the statement.

If the parties do not agree on the wording of the statement in open court, an application can be made to the judge to resolve the wording. If the parties do agree then two copies of the statement have to be lodged and are customarily read to the judge at 10.30 am in open court the following day. Where a newspaper defendant is involved it is customary, and indeed can be a term of settlement, that the making of the statement in open court is reported in the next available issue of the defendant's newspaper. It should also be made a term of any settlement that the report of the statement should be published in a position of agreed prominence. Similarly in the case of a broadcast, it should be a term of settlement that the statement in court or an agreed resumé of it, is broadcast at the beginning or end of the relevant programme

There is a provision, rarely invoked, that where a defendant will not apologise, but the plaintiff accepts a sum of money paid into court, the plaintiff can make a statement in which the defendant does not join.

Example

Honeyford v Commission for Racial Equality (1991), unreported. In that case the teacher Gordon Honeyford who was accused of racism in his school, accepted a sum of money by way of a payment out of court from the Commission for Racial Equality. A statement was read in open court but the Commission did not join in the statement.

Costs

The award of costs at the end of a trial is at the judge's discretion, under s 31 of the Supreme Court Act 1961. The award will normally follow the verdict, unless there are special circumstances such as a payment in. The award will be of the party's taxed costs and generally after taxation, a successful party will recover about two-thirds of his costs, the balance being payable by him.

Appeal

If grounds for appeal exist, either party can lodge notice of appeal. (See Section V, Chapter 11)

Check list

Damages

(1) Has the plaintiff suffered any special damages, for example, loss of earnings because he has lost his job?

(2) Has the defendant's conduct in persisting with the publication of the libel been such that the plaintiff could claim aggravated damages? Has the publication been purely for profitable motives, and thus can the plaintiff claim exemplary or punitive damages?

(3) Is the plaintiff's reputation or his claim such that the trial might result in only a contemptuous award of damages if he is successful?

Injunctions

(1) As plaintiff must come to equity with 'clean hands'—has your client behaved entirely properly? Has he acted with all possible speed?

(2) Has the plaintiff disclosed all relevant facts on an *ex parte* application?

(3) Are the words clearly defamatory?

(4) Does the affidavit show clearly not only the exact words of the alleged libel but the reason publication is anticipated?

(5) Is there likely to be a defence of justification or qualified privilege such as to prevent the grant of an interlocutory injunction?

(6) If a permanent injunction is sought and granted at the end of the case, have all steps been taken by the defendant to see that the libel is not repeated in breach of the injunction?

Statement in open court

(1) Is the plaintiff prepared to have the libel repeated in a statement in open court?
(2) Does he wish the statement publicised other than in court?
(3) What prominence does he wish any agreed report of the statement to have?
(4) Will the defendant join in the statement?
(5) Should the order require payment out of any sums in court?
(6) Does either party wish the amount of any damages to remain confidential?

Section IV

Proceedings

In this Section, a step-by-step guide to the stages of a libel action is set out, together with models of each document or pleadings.

Proceedings for libel are normally brought within the Queen's Bench Division of the High Court, although this could change if Lord Woolf's recommendations in the Access to Justice Report are adopted. All interlocutory matters relating to a libel action are now dealt with by an assigned Master; in the case of interlocutory proceedings after the case is set down, it may be heard by the judge in charge of the jury list. Applications for a preliminary ruling go to the judge.

Interrogatories and answers
   Settlement
Order
Statement in open court
   Solicitor/council for the plaintiff
   Solicitor/counsel for the defendant
   Solicitor/counsel for the plaintiff

Chapter 10

Pleadings

Example of stages in a libel action

Publication of the alleged libel

Plaintiff	**Defendant**
Letter before action	Response
Writ	Acknowledgment of service
Statement of claim	Defence [Payment into court]
Reply	[Request for further and better particulars of statement of claim] [application under RSC Ord 82, r 3A]
Request for further and better Particulars of the defence	Refusal
Summons for further and better particulars of the defence	Further and better particulars of the defence
Summons for directions	
Exchange of list of documents	Exchange of list of documents
Inspection of documents	Inspection of documents
Refusal	Request for further discovery by plaintiff

	Summons for further discovery
Supplemental list of documents [Verified by affidavit]	[Without prejudice negotiations]
Exchange of Witness Statements [Interrogatories]	Exchange of Witness Statements [Interrogatories]
Action set down for trial	
Subpoenas issued and served on witnesses	Subpoenas issued and served on witnesses
Civil Evidence Act Notices	Civil Evidence Act Notices

Then either
Trial

Judgment for the plaintiff Damages Costs	Application by defendant for Stay pending appeal
Or	
Appeal	Judgment for the defendant with costs
Or	

Settlement
Statement in open court
[Payment out of money in court]
Record withdrawn

Examples

Letter before action

In the letter before action details should be set out concerning the plaintiff, his position and his standing in the community. The letter should then out details of the alleged libel. The medium should be stated, for example, if it was television or newspaper; or if the publication was as a result of an interview or there was any prior discussion with the plaintiff and he was misled as to what was to be published, this also should be mentioned. The letter should then set out the correct facts and point out the seriousness of the alleged libel and its likely effect on the personal, private and professional life of the proposed plaintiff.

Publication or broadcast of an immediate apology, retraction or withdrawal with similar prominence to the article complained of should be requested together with an undertaking not to repeat the alleged libel, proposals for compensation and an indemnity for costs. A statement in open court can also be requested.

It is customary to ask for the name and address of solicitors who will accept service of proceedings, since the issue of a writ is a prerequisite for a statement in open court. It is also important to remember that the letter before action and the letter of response (see 'Letter of response' below) will be among the first documents to be read to the judge and jury and they should be drafted with this audience in mind.

As an example, an examination can be made of the following report in the local newspaper, the *Littlefold Gazette*.

> Mr X at the council meeting vigorously supported the proposal that Kutprice, the megastore, should be allowed to develop in the Market Square of Littlefold in the Wold. No reference was made to the fact that Mr X's wife is the owner of Smith and Brown Quality Goods, the store which at present dominates the eastern side of Market Square. The green light for the proposed development will undoubtedly benefit the property owners in and around Market Square.

Example A

Your client Mr X calls to see you. The facts are that:

(1) Neither his wife nor anybody associated with him has any interest in Smith and Brown nor any local interest which will benefit from the cut price store.

(2) He strenuously opposed the grant of planning permission to Kutprice.

(3) Since the article was published, his fellow councillors have questioned his integrity and he has been ostracised at his local golf club.

The article is defamatory in that it implies Mr X abused his position for the purpose of private gain and that he was in breach of council regulations by not declaring an interest. He has been identified by name and the matter was published on the front page of the local paper. The letter before action should set out Mr X's long years of service to the community as a councillor. The alleged libel should be referred to, the correct facts pointed out and the letter should insist on publication of a correction and apology to be published on the front page of the next issue of the local paper, damages, an undertaking not to repeat the untrue allegation and a statement in open court and reimbursement of costs.

Example B: your client is the local paper

On receipt of the letter from Mr X's solicitors it will be necessary to show that the report was a fair and accurate report of a council meeting and therefore publication of that part of the article is privileged subject to explanation or contradiction under Sched 1, Pts I and II to the Defamation Act 1996 (see Section II, Chapter 5). If the reporter has made a mistake about whether Mr X opposed the proposal, then a correction should be published in the next available issue in a position of reasonable prominence and without prejudice negotiations to dispose of the matter on that basis entered into immediately.

With regard to the rest of the article, if the facts are wrong then similarly an immediate correction must be sought. If however, enquiries reveal that Mrs X did own Smith and Brown Quality Goods until a year ago when the ownership was transferred to a company in which she and Mr X were the only shareholders, then even though Mr X opposed the application, the newspaper could mount a limited defence of justification since he did not declare an interest and indeed could conceivably be opposed to the council granting a licence to Kutprice because he believes a higher offer may be made by a competing megastore, Supervalue, which would be of greater benefit to the company owning Smith and Brown Quality Goods.

On a practical note, it is frequently the case that a letter before action prepared at speed in response to pressure from the client may not cover all the areas which need to be dealt with in the statement of claim. When instructions are prepared to counsel to settle the statement of claim, other matters may come to light or more detail may be given which may alter or expand the alleged meanings. Although reference may be made to the difference between the letter before action and the statement of claim at any trial, it is not a matter which should cause a serious problem. In certain circumstances, it may be more important to get in a swift claim on behalf of the plaintiff to prevent a repetition of the libel and seek an immediate apology than to delay while obtaining all the signed statements that might be required by counsel before settling the statement of claim. At all events this letter should be drafted with great care even if done at speed since as stated this will be the first detail which the judge and jury hear about the plaintiff's claim. All subsequent correspondence should also be drafted with that eventual audience in mind.

Example C: newspaper

Editor
Daily News
Dear Sir

'Our client, the distinguished consultant, has instructed us in connection with an article which appeared in the *Daily News* 10 November 1995 under the headline "Consultant involved with Call Girl".

This article contains a number of gravely defamatory statements about our client who is an eminent and highly respected senior member of his profession. The personal attack on our client must be one of the most serious libels imaginable. Your article states that the General Medical Council had been "hoodwinked by a fairy tale" implying that our client had been dishonest in his dealings at the time when the true facts were known to your reporter. Not content with publishing these grave libels about our client, you have also made it appear that he has criticised his own governing body which is calculated to cause him considerable embarrassment and again, as known to you, is completely untrue.

It is hard to imagine a more damaging series of libels of our client which are calculated to cause him serious and lasting damage both in his public and private life reflecting as they do on his integrity, his honesty, his professional competence and his motives. We have advised our client that he is entitled to substantial damages for libel together with aggravated damages, since firstly at no time did you check any of the so-called "facts" in this story with our client before publication and secondly because the libels have been published at a time when you knew them to be untrue.

The purpose of this letter is to invite you to publish a prominent, full and unqualified apology in terms to be agreed in the next issue of your newspaper, to pay our client substantial damages to attempt to compensate him for the damage your publication has caused him and to reimburse him in full for his legal costs. We shall also require an undertaking that you will not repeat any of the libels complained of either in your newspaper or by way of syndication. As in any event our client will require a statement in open court, we are today issuing a writ and should be obliged if you would let us know the name and address of your solicitors who will accept service of proceedings on your behalf.

Yours faithfully'

Example D: television
The Controller
TV North Central
Dear Sir
'Our clients, General Sausage Company and Mr Dick Jones, the Managing Director, have instructed us in connection with the forthcoming broadcast of *Facts on Trial*. Our clients have passed to us the letter to you from the Sausage Manufacturers Association of 19 January and your response of 28 January.

We consider it a matter of regret that you were not willing to supply a copy of the programme to the Sausage Manufacturers Association before transmission to enable them to review the accuracy of the contents. The purpose of this letter is to notify you that we are instructed to watch the programme to be broadcast on 8 December on our clients' behalf. Should it contain any matter which reflects on any of our clients, either by way of defamation or slander of goods, our clients will not hesitate to take the appropriate legal action. In the event of any such action we shall, of course, draw to the attention of the court the fact that you did not avail yourself of the opportunity to check the accuracy of the programme before transmission.

Yours faithfully'

Example E: producer

AB Cloggs
Producer
Dear Sir
'Further to our letter to you of [   ] we have, as instructed, watched the broadcast "Sausages—A Serious Problem" on 8 February. Your broadcast contained a number of statements of defamatory and misleading nature calculated to cause our clients great damage. To name but a few, it was stated that our clients used unhygienic working practices in preparing their sausages; that their sausages contained below the legal requirement of meat and that the meat used was from parts of animals that would normally be abandoned in the abattoir. These are but a small selection of the many damaging statements.

At the time of writing, namely within 12 hours of the broadcast, our clients have had substantial cancellations of orders from major supermarkets, all of whom have cited your broadcast as the reason for the cancellation of the orders.

The purpose of this letter is to notify you that our clients require a right of reply by way of the apology enclosed to be broadcast immediately before this weekend's *Facts on Trial* programme. In the meantime all our clients' rights are reserved.

Yours faithfully'

Letter of response

This letter should refute allegations made by the plaintiff. It should set out the true facts including any relevant factors concerning the circumstances of how the publication of the defamatory statement came to be made, for example, if it was based on an interview with the proposed plaintiff. It should indicate with sufficient detail what will be the basis of any likely defence and should state that the matter will be defended if that is the case. If the letter is sent by solicitors on behalf of the proposed defendant it should confirm that instructions have been received to accept service of any proceedings.

In certain circumstances it may be appropriate for the proposed defendant's advisors to draft a letter for the client to send direct. This can also be useful where it is apparent that there may not be a defence in which case a prompt offer of apology (see 'Apology' below) from the client may defuse the situation. In any event, when the letter before action is received, and regrettably it is not always the case that such a letter is received, a holding letter stating that the matter is being investigated should immediately be sent either by the client direct or by those advising him.

Example F: letter of response

Dear Sir
'We have now had an opportunity of investigating the matters raised in your letter of [   ].

Your client has complained that the statements in the issue of the *Daily News* of 13 June 1996 under the headline "Raunchy Ron Fired" are defamatory of your client. The article contained an account of how your client was asked to leave the film set of *Whistling in the Dark* where he had been an assistant director because of what were described as "artistic differences".

We are satisfied from the evidence which we have collated that firstly our clients were entirely justified in asking your client to leave the film set; secondly, that your client had had three warnings about his behaviour on and off the set (the last two of which were in writing) in relation to both his conduct with the female members of the cast and cavalier attitude in relation to expenses; thirdly that your client then using the name of Den Tate was convicted of fraud in 1986 for defrauding his then employer ANT Films Ltd of £25,000; and fourthly, that your client was summarily dismissed from the set of *Little Children* in 1973 because of his behaviour with a female member of the cast.

In these circumstances should your client issue proceedings for libel we are satisfied that we have a complete defence of justification. Our clients have instructed us that any such action will be vigorously defended. We confirm that we have instructions to accept service of proceedings.

Yours faithfully'

Apology

Example G: typical apologies

Television: 'In last week's *Facts on Trial* we made certain statements concerning the General Sausage Company and its Managing Director, Mr Dick Jones.

In particular we alleged that the company and Mr Jones did not comply with appropriate legislation. We now accept that, contrary to our report, the company fully complies with all legislation concerning hygiene and meat quantity, and indeed that its sausages recently won the International Sausage Quality Prize. We much regret the broadcast and apologise unreservedly to the company and to Mr Jones.'

Magazine: 'In the *Gazette* of 11 May 1995 we published a photograph of three barristers, including Ms Susie Cooper, in the context of a news article on sexual harassment. The photograph, obtained from a library source, was not intended to imply that the individuals appearing in it were involved in any way in the story concerned and we fully accept that Ms Susie Cooper has not been connected in any way with any of the allegations reported in the article.

We wish to apologise unreservedly to Ms Susie Cooper for any distress or embarrassment that the publication of her photograph has caused her.'

Periodical: 'Jo Bloggs, and his publishers, Exciting Books Ltd, wish to apologise unreservedly to the crime novelist, Fred Smith, whose twentieth whodunit, *Under the Stairs*, appears from First Publications Ltd this summer.

References to Mr Smith in Mr Bloggs' book *The Spiral Nightmare* might be judged to have impugned Mr Smith's integrity, and to have questioned his standing as a successful writer of popular fiction. Such imputations are now acknowledged to have been made carelessly and to have no foundation whatsoever.'

Newspaper: 'On 22 November last year we carried a story indicating that Mr Tiny Tim, Chairman of Tiny Tim Ltd had been mentioned in connection with a vacancy at the Whigs for Socialism Central Office. It was claimed that a senior official within that office was likely to veto such an appointment because according to his aide he regarded Mr Tiny Tim as "beneath contempt". We now understand that no such statement was made and apologise to Mr Tiny Tim for this untrue story.'

Example
Writ

IN THE HIGH COURT OF JUSTICE   1996 C No 1234
QUEEN'S BENCH DIVISION

B E T W E E N :   R CUTLIFT ESQ   *Plaintiff*
                              and
                              (1) DAILY NEWS LTD
                              (2) JOE BLOGGS
                              (3) C SCOOP   *Defendants*

WRIT OF SUMMONS

TO THE DEFENDANTS DAILY NEWS LTD, JOE BLOGGS and C SCOOP
whose registered office is situate at One Docklands Avenue, London
THIS WRIT OF SUMMONS has been issued against you by the above-
named plaintiff in respect of the claim set out overleaf.

Within 14 days after the service of this writ on you, counting the day of
service, you must either satisfy the claim or return to the court's office
mentioned below the accompanying acknowledgment of service stating
therein whether you intend to contest these proceedings.

If you fail to satisfy the claim or to return the acknowledgment within the
time stated, or if you return the acknowledgment without stating therein an
intention to contest the proceedings, the plaintiff may proceed with the action
and judgment may be entered against you forthwith without further notice.

Issued from the Central Office of the High Court this ..... day of .... .

Note: This writ may not be served later than four calendar months (*or, if
leave is required to effect service out of the jurisdiction, six months*) beginning with that date unless renewed by order of the court.

IMPORTANT

Directions for acknowledgment of service are given with the accompanying
form.

And the plaintiff claims:
(1) damages for libel;
(2) an injunction to restrain the defendants and each of them whether by
     themselves, their directors, servants or agents or otherwise howsoever
     from further publishing the said or any similar words defamatory of the
     plaintiff.This writ was issued by ....
     Solicitors for the said plaintiff whose address is ......

At paragraph (1):

In relation to a newspaper where the writ may be directed to the company owning the newspaper (the first defendant), the editor (the third defendant), and any journalist (the second defendant) bylined, the endorsement would say:

'(1) Damages for libel contained in an article headed "Floozy runs off with millions" written and published or caused to be published by the second defendant and published or caused to be published by the first and third defendants in the *Daily News* issue dated 12 March 1995.'

In relation to a television broadcast:

'(1) Damages for libel contained in a broadcast published by the defendant in a programme entitled *Facts on Trial* on [DATE]'.

In relation to a book against the publisher and author:

'(1) Damages for libel appearing on pages six to nine of the book entitled *The Missing Millions*, written and published or caused to be published by the second defendant and published or caused to be published by the first defendant.'

The injunction as requested at (2) above would remain the same.

Statement of claim

In preparing the statement of claim care should be taken to set out those parts of the article, publication or transcript of which complaint is made. The plaintiff must then set out the meanings upon which he relies and which he alleges are defamatory of him. He must also set out the reason why the passage has been understood to refer to him if he is not named. So, for example, in a book in which the plaintiff was named in one passage but not another, it would be necessary to plead both passages and to set out the reasons for the claim that a reasonable reader would impute the plaintiff's name into the second passage.

The statement of claim must also state that by reason of the publication complained of the plaintiff has been caused great personal distress and embarrassment, has been gravely injured in his reputation and has been brought into public scandal, odium and contempt. In addition under RSC Ord 82 it is necessary to plead all facts and matters relied on by a plaintiff in support of the damages claim. The statement of claim should include a request for an order that the libel should not be repeated as well as a claim for damages and costs or ancillary relief.

Example

IN THE HIGH COURT OF JUSTICE   1996 C No 1234
QUEEN'S BENCH DIVISION

B E T W E E N: R CUTLIFT ESQ   *Plaintiff*
                                and
                        (1) DAILY NEWS
                        (2) JOE BLOGGS
                        (3) C SCOOP   *Defendants*

STATEMENT OF CLAIM

The statement of claim will incorporate the following:

Paragraph one will contain details of the plaintiff, including particulars of his reputation which have been affected by the libel or slander, for example, 'the plaintiff is a distinguished surgeon, a member of the College of Surgeons who has been in private practice since 19...'; or in the case of a corporate plaintiff 'the plaintiff is in the business of process packaging and sells crisps under the name "Susie's Crisps"; or 'the plaintiff is a public limited company which carries on business both as a publisher and as a supplier of printing services. The second and third plaintiffs are the Managing Director and the Financial Director'.

Paragraph two of the statement of claim will normally state the identity of the defendants, eg, 'the first defendant is the proprietor of the *Daily News*, the second defendant is the editor and the third defendant is the journalist employed by them,' or 'the defendant operates a national television known as Channel 9 which broadcasts programmes for general reception throughout the jurisdiction'; 'the defendant is the proprietor of the *Daily News* newspaper which has a large and influential circulation primarily throughout the jurisdiction of this honourable court'.

Paragraph three of the statement of claim will then detail the date and occasion when the alleged libel was published with sufficient detail to identify the article or broadcast. It should be stated that the words were defamatory or that they were spoken about the plaintiff. The defamatory words should then be set out after the words 'the following defamatory words of the plaintiff ...' . Where not all the defamatory words are used, for example, only part of an article or part of a book or part of a broadcast, it is customary to indicate that the words are not continuous. If it is a book it should be stated that 'the plaintiff will refer to the whole of the said book for the full context of the words complained of'.

Paragraph four of the statement of claim will set out 'the said words in their natural and ordinary meaning which were understood to mean' and then set out the meanings, for example:
(1) That the plaintiff was responsible for injuries to patients.
(2) That the plaintiff had operated negligently and incompetently.
(3) That the plaintiff had sought to deceive his governing body when the matter was investigated.

Paragraph five of the statement of claim will state 'by reason of the matters aforesaid, the plaintiff has been severely damaged in his character and reputation and has been caused considerable distress and embarrassment.' In the case of a company: 'that the first plaintiff has been seriously injured in its business reputation and goodwill and has suffered loss and damage.'

By virtue of RSC Ord 82, r 3 the plaintiff must set out particulars of all facts and matters relied on for general damages and also must serve particulars for aggravated or exemplary damages as follows:
(1) general 'In support of his claim for damages the plaintiff will rely on the following facts and matters ... '
(2) aggravated 'In support of his claim for general and/or aggravated damages ...'
(3) exemplary 'In support of his claim for general and/or exemplary damages ...'. (See Section III, Chapter 9.)

Paragraph six will conclude that: 'unless restrained by this honourable court, the defendants and each of them will further publish or cause to be published the same or similar words defamatory of the plaintiff.

And the plaintiff claims (against the defendants and each of them):
(1) Damages for (if appropriate "including aggravated damages") libel;
(2) Special damages—if appropriate; and
(3) An injunction to restrain the defendants and each of them (in the case of a defendant company by its officers, servants, agents or howsoever otherwise and in the case of individuals by themselves, their servants, agents or howsoever otherwise from further publishing the said or similar libels of the plaintiffs (plaintiff).'

Example
Defence

IN THE HIGH COURT OF JUSTICE   1996 C No 1234
QUEEN'S BENCH DIVISION

B E T W E E N :   R CUTLIFT ESQ   *Plaintiff*
                              and
                         (1) DAILY NEWS
                         (2) JOE BLOGGS
                         (3) C SCOOP   *Defendants*

DEFENCE

(1) Admit paragraph 1 of the statement of claim (this normally relates to the plaintiff).

(2) Admit that the defendants are newspapers (publishers) (television company) but not necessarily the extent of any alleged circulation or readership.

(3) Admit publication of the words complained of.

(4) Deny that the words are defamatory.

(5) Deny that they refer or were understood to refer or capable of being understood to refer to the plaintiff as alleged:

It is denied that the words complained of bore or were understood to bear or are capable of bearing the meanings pleaded in paragraph six of the statement of claim or any of them or any meanings defamatory of the plaintiff.

It is customary at this part of the pleading, where only part of an article, broadcast, or book is relied on as defamatory, for the defendant to draw the court's attention to the remainder of the article and for the content to be taken into account:

The defendants will rely on the full text of the said article (broadcast) (book) for its proper content and effect.

These are purely formal defences. Substantive defences follow:

(6) *Fair Comment*   'Further or in the alternative, the words complained of were fair comment on a matter of public interest.'

(7) *Justification*   Where the defendant does not accept the plaintiff's meaning, he should set out the meaning or meanings which he does accept and plead the truth of those meanings as follows:

in the alternative if and insofar as the words complained of bore the meaning that ... they were true in substance and in fact.

Further or in the alternative, the words complained of were true in substance and in fact.

(8) *Qualified Privilege* 'Further or in the alternative, the words complained of were published on an occasion of qualified privilege.'

In all cases particulars of the facts and matters relied on to support the justification and fair comment pleas, or to show that the occasion was one of qualified privilege, must be set out. The defendant can also set out the meanings which he intends to justify. Where a defence of justification is pleaded in the alternative to fair comment, the particulars of the facts to support it will normally be the same as those which support the fair comment. In cases of both fair comment and justification, the defendant must give particulars stating which words are alleged to be statements of fact and the facts and matters relied upon in support of the allegation that the words are true.

(9) At this part of the defence, it is customary to insert that the defendants will, if necessary, rely on ss 5 and/or 6 of the Defamation Act 1952 relating to justification and fair comment.

(10) In relation to the claim for damages it is normal to deny and not admit the particulars of damages or a general allegation and in relation to exemplary or aggravated damages it can also be denied that the particulars are capable of supporting such a claim for exemplary or aggravated damages.

Example

IN THE HIGH COURT OF JUSTICE 1995 A No 3456
QUEEN'S BENCH DIVISION

B E T W E E N :   (1) ANT LTD   *Plaintiffs*
                (2) ALBERT BROWN
                and
                DAILY CLARION LTD   *Defendant*

DEFENCE

(1) No admissions have been made to paragraph one of the statement of claim (this is effectively putting the plaintiffs to proof of the statements they make concerning themselves).

(2) Save that no admissions are made as to the size of circulation of the *Daily Clarion*, it is admitted that the defendant caused to be published the words set out in paragraph two.

(3) It is denied that the said words referred to were understood to refer to the plaintiffs or either of them. Further it is denied that the words were defamatory of the plaintiffs or either of them.

(4) It is denied that the words bore or were understood to bear or were capable of bearing the meanings set out in paragraph four of the statement of claim or any defamatory meaning of them or any of the plaintiffs or either of them.

(5) Further, or in the alternative, if and insofar as the words complained of bore the following meaning or meanings:

    (a) that the first plaintiff improperly took advantage of his position as Finance Director; and

    (b) that the plaintiffs knew or ought to have known that ANT Ltd and DEF Ltd were loss making;

the defendant contends that they are true in substance and in fact. If and insofar as may be necessary the defendant will rely on s 5 of the Defamation Act 1952.

Particulars

(1) At all material times the first plaintiff was Finance Director of ANT Ltd. In February 1993, he instructed the firm's accountants to prepare a valuation of the shares and provided them with estimates of pre-tax profits of £1m for ANT Ltd and £1.5m for its subsidiary, DEF Ltd. As the plaintiff knew or ought to have

known, those estimates were very substantial over-estimates of the likely profit. ANT Ltd reported a pre-tax loss for the year ended 1992 of £683,000 and DEF Ltd reported a loss for that year of £220,000.

(2)   Those over-estimates of likely profit were on the instruction of the plaintiff conveyed by internal memo dated 29 February 1990 to the accountants who were directed to use those over-estimates as the basis for the share valuation.

Where a defamatory innuendo is pleaded, the appropriate paragraph would be 'insofar as the said words mean that the plaintiffs were guilty of criminal fraud, the defendant denies the innuendo'.

Meanings

It is open to the defendant, after service of the statement of claim, to apply to the court under Ord 82, r 3(A) to have tried by a judge as a preliminary issue before trial, whether the words set out in a particular paragraph of the statement of claim are reasonably capable of bearing the meanings pleaded in the statement of claim. If this is tried as a preliminary issue and as a result a paragraph in the statement of claim is deleted, this will obviously save the expense of leaving such pleadings unamended and having a paragraph struck out at trial.

Reply

Where a defence has pleaded fair comment or qualified privilege, the reply will contain the facts and matters on which the plaintiff relies to support an allegation of malice against the defendant to defeat those two defences. As explained previously, where there is a plea of justification and fair comment, the defendant has to give particulars as to which are statements of fact and which are comments. He must then set out the facts and matters relied on to support the truth of those facts. Under Ord 82, r 3(2A) the plaintiff must then serve a reply specifically admitting or denying any allegation raised by the defendant and specifying any fact or matter upon which he relies in opposition to the defendant's allegation. This recent change in the RSC is again designed to enable each party to identify at an early stage of the proceedings the precise case to be met.

It therefore prevent the defendants being ambushed by the plaintiff at the trial denying the truth of the matters pleaded by the defence. It can also in practice, have the effect of forcing the plaintiff to face what may be deficiencies in his own case. Not all clients may have fully briefed their advisors so that a defence alleging the truth of certain of the defamatory matters may force a settlement.

Example

IN THE HIGH COURT OF JUSTICE   1995 A No 3456
QUEEN'S BENCH DIVISION

B E T W E E N :   (1) ANT LTD   *Plaintiffs*
                         (2) ALBERT BROWN
                              and
                         (3) DAILY CLARION LTD   *Defendant*

REPLY

(1) The plaintiff joins issue with the defence save insofar as the same consists of omissions and in the respects pleaded below.

(2) It is denied that the words complained of bore or were intended to bear the meanings pleaded in paragraph four of the defence. The meaning was as pleaded in the statement of claim.

(3) As to the Particulars under paragraph four, the plaintiff pleads as follows:

4.1 It is admitted that the first plaintiff was the Finance Director of ANT Ltd and that he instructed the firm's accountants to prepare a valuation of the shares. It is denied that the plaintiff was aware that the estimate was an over estimate.

4.2 It is denied that the plaintiff had conveyed an internal memo to the accountants.

4.3 The statement was published maliciously.

4.4 The facts and matters which are now pleaded as comment, were not the facts and matters before the defendant when it wrote the article complained of.

Further and better particulars

The purpose of pleadings, and indeed Ord 82, r 3(2A), is to define as precisely as possible the meanings and facts in issue between the parties. It is therefore not uncommon in libel proceedings to have extensive requests for further and better particulars of the statement of claim and the defence. If inadequate particulars are given, a strike out application can be made. In the case of *McDonalds v Morris and Steel* (above), where a strike out application was issued because it was alleged that the particulars of justification were inadequate, certain precise guidelines concerning the requirements of particulars were laid out. (See Section II, Chapter 3.)

Summons for directions

The issue for the summons for directions by the plaintiff is similar to other forms of litigation. An Order for Directions is sought for laying down a timetable for discovery, exchange of witness statements and setting down the action to take the case up to trial. In libel, a jury will be assigned to the case automatically. Occasionally a judge can be asked by either side to rule because the technical nature of the claim is considered inappropriate for a jury, for example, in *Upjohn v BBC* (above) involving as it did analysis of the medical properties of the Halcion drug (see Section III, Chapter 9) there was no jury. Neither was there a jury in the case of *McDonalds v Morris and Steel* (above) which involved technical evidence.

Mitigation

On occasions it may be that the defendant may not have sufficient evidence to mount a plea of justification or fair comment, notwithstanding the provisions of ss 5 and 6 of the Defamation Act 1952. In those circumstances, it may be appropriate to plead various facts and matters in mitigation, for example, if a right of reply was offered and rejected, that could be pleaded in mitigation, or if an apology was offered and/or published.

Payment into court

A payment into court is a useful weapon in libel proceedings especially if it is made early in the proceedings and the cost to the defendant will only be the interest on the money in court. This can put considerable pressure on a plaintiff particularly having regard to the costs of taking a matter through to trial. The payment into court is not known to the judge or jury and the plaintiff will normally have 21 days within which to accept. If it is not accepted within that period and the plaintiff then goes on to recover the same amount at trial or less, then he must pay the costs from the date of the payment in. This is because had he taken the money out of court the matter could have been finalised at that date.

The defendant can also add to a payment into court at any stage and even during a trial additional payments can be made into court. (See Section II, Chapter 7.)

Exchange of witness statements

The new provisions under RSC Ord 38 for the exchange of witness statements are designed again to limit the surprise element at trial. The intention to order the exchange of witness statements was obviously to limit the costs of trial by finding the areas of fact which were common to both parties and limiting the time taken by witnesses in giving evidence in court.

However, it has unfortunately also had the effect of increasing the costs because of the necessity of having counsel's full advice on witness statements before exchange. In a number of cases, the witness statements can be ordered to stand as evidence-in-chief. Indeed the interim report on 'Access to Justice' by Lord Woolf has recommended limitations on live cross-examination where witness statements exist. If these recommendations are adopted, while it will obviously speed up trials, it will severely limit the ability to test a witness in court. An additional complication is that frequently further information is discovered shortly before trial or does not become available until very late or even during the trial itself, and then supplemental witness statements have to be served.

Discovery

Both parties to a libel action should be instructed at the beginning of the action that all relevant documentation should be retained and that no documents should be destroyed which may be relevant to the proceedings. As in any litigation, meticulous discovery can frequently be a deciding factor in a case. It may either be because the extent of the documentation at the discovery stage renders it uneconomic to continue or because the documentation itself reveals substantial flaws in one party's case. Generally speaking in the case of a newspaper, reporter's notes will be disclosable. In the case of a book, the published edition will normally be the only version disclosable. If, however, there is a question of malice, then the manuscript and any amendment to it may be disclosable.

It is established that discovery cannot normally precede particulars of justification but reference should be made to the *McDonalds* case for the full ruling (see Section II, Chapter 3). Claims for special damages and exemplary damages by a plaintiff can broaden the scope of discovery considerably. A claim for special damages can mean a company's accounts will be disclosable and a claim for exemplary damages can mean that a company's boardroom minutes are disclosable.

Examples

In the case brought by Neil Hamilton MP and Ian Greer Associates against the *Guardian* newspaper, which was abandoned spectacularly the day before the trial, the special damages claim of £10m by Ian Greer Associates meant that all the company's accounts were disclosable. It was subsequently revealed in the press after the case had been abandoned that the accounts showed payments to a number of MPs by Ian Greer Accociates, including several Labour MPs.

In *Western Provident v Norwich Union* (1995), unreported, the defendants' allegedly defamatory internal e-mails were held to be disclosable and in fact discovery of them was ordered prior to the issue of the writ.

Interrogatories and answers

A similar comment applies to interrogatories. Interrogatories and notices to admit facts can also be a way of defining the issues and putting pressure on the opposing side before trial.

Example

IN THE HIGH COURT OF JUSTICE   1996 C No 1234
QUEEN'S BENCH DIVISION

B E T W E E N :	R CUTLIFT ESQ	*Plaintiff*
	and	
	(1) DAILY NEWS	
	(2) JOE BLOGGS	
	(3) C SCOOP	*Defendants*

INTERROGATORIES

Interrogatories to the third defendant:

(1) Did you in or about July 1992 speak the words set out in paragraph 3 of the statement of claim or words to the like effect?

(2) If the answer of the first interrogatory is yes, then: did you speak the said words in the presence and hearing of the second defendant and if so where?

(3) Did you on or about July 1992 write the article complained of and send it electronically to the first defendant?

(4) If the answer to the third interrogatory is yes, then: did you send by fax to the plaintiff a copy of the article containing all or some of the words set out in the statement of claim or words to the like effect?

Settlement

It should be borne in mind that a large proportion of libel actions are eventually settled on terms which can include an agreed statement in open court. Sometimes there is a form of consent order dismissing the action, which means that no fresh proceedings can be issued by the plaintiff because the matter has been finalised. Alternatively there can be a consent order in which the action is discontinued or a claim withdrawn, which means that unless it has been specifically agreed, it would be open to the plaintiff to issue fresh proceedings within the limitation period. Finally, a settlement can be secured simply by an exchange of letters between the parties' solicitors.

A sample order is set out below to be used if the matter should be settled.

Example
Order

IN THE HIGH COURT OF JUSTICE   1995A No 3456
QUEEN'S BENCH DIVISION

BETWEEN   (1) ANT LTD
                         (2) ALBERT BROWN   *Plaintiffs*
                               and
                         DAILY CLARION LTD   *Defendant*

ORDER

UPON the parties agreeing terms
    IT IS ORDERED that this action be dismissed with no order as to costs.
    OR
    UPON the parties agreeing terms
    AND BY CONSENT
    IT IS ORDERED that the action be withdrawn with no order as to costs.

Example
Statement in open court

IN THE HIGH COURT OF JUSTICE   1997 F 456
QUEEN'S BENCH DIVISION

B E T W E E N :   EDWARD BROWN FOOT   *Plaintiff*
                              and
                      DAILY CLARION LTD   *Defendant*

STATEMENT IN OPEN COURT

Solicitor/counsel for the plaintiff

The plaintiff is a prominent and distinguished Consultant who has been in private practice since 1969 and was for over 20 years the senior partner of the Harpole Street practice at No 5 Harpole Street. He is a past President of the Royal Association of Chiropodists and a frequent contributor of distinguished articles to the *Lancet*.

In the issue of the *Daily Clarion* of the 13 January 1994 under the headline 'Chiropodist Fails to Save Foot' the defendant published an article severely criticising the plaintiff for failure to prevent a minor injury becoming gangrenous resulting in the amputation of the patient's foot. The words were highly defamatory and totally untrue, in that the incident had never happened. The plaintiff had at no time treated the patient featured in the article and had indeed written an article in the *Lancet* himself condemning the treatment, given by a doctor abroad, which had resulted in the unfortunate amputation. The article has caused the plaintiff considerable distress, reflecting as it does directly on his professional competence. In his personal life, both he and his family have been subject to considerable hurt and embarrassment. The defendant, through his counsel, is here today to withdraw unreservedly each and every allegation against the plaintiff contained in the article and to apologise. In addition, the defendant has agreed to pay substantial damages to the plaintiff and to reimburse him in respect of all his legal costs. In the circumstances the plaintiff is content that he has been wholly vindicated and he is prepared now to let this matter rest.

Solicitor/counsel for the defendant

On behalf of the publishers of the *Daily Clarion* I endorse everything my (learned) friend has told the court. The defendant accepts that the matters written in this article were wholly untrue and constituted a serious libel on the plaintiff's personal and professional reputation. The defendant is pleased to withdraw these allegations unreservedly and to apologise to the plaintiff for the hurt and embarrassment which he has been caused.

Solicitor/counsel for the plaintiff

In the circumstances I need only ask for leave for the record to be withdrawn (and for payment out of the money in court).

Section V

Recent Developments and General Advice

In this Section Chapter 11 examines recent developments in the law of libel with a particular reference to: the Defamation Act 1996; Internet libel; the effect of Europe on the domestic libel law of the UK; and appeal procedures. It will conclude in Chapter 12 with general advice in relation to libel actions.

Chapter 11—Recent Developments

Defamation Act 1996
    Defences
    Procedural changes
    Evidential changes
Europe
    Damages
    Forum
Internet
Appeal
    Courts and Legal Services Act 1990, s 8
    Court of Appeal Elton John Guidelines 1995
    European Court of Human Rights

Chapter 12—General Advice

Tactics
Pre-publication advice
Speed

Chapter 11

Recent Developments

In this Chapter the following recent developments in libel law will be examined:
- (a) the Defamation Act 1996;
- (b) Europe
- (c) Internet; and
- (d) appeal procedures.

Defamation Act 1996

Most practitioners and probably a number of members of the public would agree that reforms to the libel laws are well overdue. In 1975, the Faulks Committee made extensive recommendations which were supported by practitioners, but which unfortunately were never implemented. In 1990, Lord Justice Neil was asked to chair a committee to look at practice and procedure in defamation. The Committee's report in 1991 made a number of recommendations, as a result of which, a draft Defamation Bill was prepared for consultation in July 1995. The final Bill received the Royal Assent in 1996. The reforms in the Act fall into three main areas:
- (a) defences;
- (b) procedural changes; and
- (c) evidential changes.

Defences

Responsibility for publication
Section 1 of the Act provides an entirely new defence for a person who can show that he is not primarily responsible for publication and took reasonable care. At first sight this appears to extend the defence of innocent dissemination but it is, in fact, both more specific and more circumscribed than that defence. A defendant has to show that:
- (a) he was not the author, editor or publisher;

(b) he took reasonable care; and

(c) he did not know and had no reason to believe that what he did caused or contributed to publication of the defamatory statement.

This has been widely described as the Internet defence and under s 1(3) there is a specific provision covering those involved in processing data through an electronic medium or operating a communications system. The section does appear to be likely to achieve a defence for those involved in transmitting material across the Internet which they have no reason to know is defamatory. In addition s 1(5) of the Defamation Act 1996 provides that a court may consider:

(a) the extent of the defendant's responsibility for the content of the statement or the decision to publish;

(b) the nature of the publication; and

(c) the previous content.

Example

To date there has been only one known defamation action in the UK in respect of e-mail (*PC Eggleton v Asda* (1995), unreported) . In that case, following his complaint over some faulty goods PC Eggleton found out by chance that an e-mail had been broadcast throughout the Asda stores' network accusing him of fraud. He sued for libel on the publication within the stores' group and the matter was settled.

It is expected that as the use of e-mail becomes more widespread both within offices and linking offices, libel actions are likely to follow. Proof of publication would, of course, be required. While an e-mail message can be removed from the screen, computers can retain the message within the system, and it can be produced, for example, on discovery. In the *Western Provident Association v Norwich Union* case (1995), unreported, as has been seen above, disclosure of allegedly defamatory e-mails passing within the defendant company was ordered prior to the issue of a writ.

Offer to make amends

Section 2 of the Defamation Act 1996 provides an up-dated offer of amends defence. It will be recalled (see Section II, Chapter 6) that the original offer of amends defence under s 4 of the Defamation Act 1952 was never widely used in practice. The new defence is designed to cover those cases where a defamatory statement has been published innocently by the defendant, and to simplify the procedural complications which bedevilled the 1952 Act offer of amends procedure. There is now no requirement that the offer of amends has to be made 'as soon as practicable', a restriction which led to difficulties and variations of decisions in practice as to what constituted 'as soon as practicable'. The offer, as before, must be in writing, must be stated to be under s 2 of the 1996 Act and the offer must be to:

(a) join in the publication of a suitable correction and apology;
(b) take steps to notify those to whom the defamatory statements have been published that it is defamatory; and
(c) pay the complainant compensation and costs.

An additional improvement in the offer of amends procedure from the point of view of the defendant under s 4. Subsection 3 of s 4 provides that an offer of amends can only be made if the person by whom the offer is made did not know that the statement complained of:

(a) referred to the aggrieved party or was likely to be understood as refer- ring to him; and
(b) was both false and defamatory of that party;
but it shall be presumed until the contrary is shown that he did not know and had no reason to believe that was the case.

This means that the onus of showing that the statement was known by the defendant to refer to him and to be false and defamatory shifts to the plaintiff. This could be a significant factor in making the offer of amends procedure widely used by a defendant.

The offer to pay compensation is a new provision which could be likely, in practice, to deter a defendant from relying on this defence. While s 3 of the Act provides that if the party complaining decides to accept the offer 'the amount to be paid by way of compensation shall be determined on the same principles as damages in defamation proceed- ings', this somewhat vague statement is unlikely to be reassuring in the case, for example, of a newspaper relying on an offer of amends.

Unusually under s 3, the court not only has power if the parties can- not agree on compensation, to determine the amount of any compensa- tion but can also determine the amount of any costs to be awarded. At one time there was a proposal that the court should also have the power to direct the manner and publication of any apology but this was seen as an interference with the right of the free press. The court is now able to take into account the manner of an apology in assessing the compensa- tion. The court may reduce or increase the compensation taking into account: 'the suitability of the correction, the sufficiency of the apology and whether the manner of their publication was reasonable in the cir- cumstances'.

A second improvement on the previous offer of amends procedure under s 4 is the provision to provide a qualified offer. In many cases, the defamatory statements may contain a number of meanings, for only some of which may be appropriate for the defendant to rely on an offer of amends. A defendant can therefore make a qualified offer of amends in respect of those defamatory statements which he claims to have made innocently, while applying another defence to the remainder.

However, a disadvantage in the 1996 Act offer is that if the defendant seeks to rely on the offer of amends as a defence, he is precluded from pleading any other defence. As has been shown (see Section IV, Chapter 10) it is common practice in defamation proceedings to rely on a number of alternative defences. Section 4 provides that the offer may be relied on in mitigation of damages whether or not it is relied on as a defence, but it does seem on the face of it to be an unnecessary restriction to prevent a defendant treating the offer of amends as an alternative defence. A situation could arise in practice where an offer of amends is made and if not accepted is then withdrawn as a defence in favour of, say, alternative pleas of fair comment, justification, or qualified privilege with the defendant keeping the offer of amends in mitigation but precluded from relying on it as a defence. On the face of it, this would seem a deterrent to invoking the procedure and costs.

Where the offer is accepted then that is an end to the proceedings. However, the judge, as a jury is specifically excluded from dealing with offers of amends, may approve the correction and apology and determine the amount of compensation and costs.

Example

An example of the difficulty of deciding compensation arose in the *Kiam v Sunday Times and Andrew Neil* (1996) *The Times*, 26 July. In that case, Victor Kiam, owner of the Remington razor company, sued the *Sunday Times* over a highly defamatory article which stated that he was being sued by the National Westminster Bank and he had applied for bankruptcy protection. Both statements were untrue and the *Sunday Times* made an open offer of amends (under the Defamation Act 1952) and published an agreed apology three weeks after the article complained of. At the trial, the jury awarded £45,000 damages and the *Sunday Times* appealed. The Court of Appeal held that the award of £45,000 for what was described as 'a widespread, grave and irresponsible assertion of insolvency against a prominent entrepreneur' was not excessive and the appeal was dismissed.

Privilege

Under s 14 of the Act, absolute privilege has been extended to cover fair and accurate reports before any UK court, before the European Court of Justice, the European Court of Human Rights and any international criminal court established by the United Nations. As in the 1952 Act, the

Schedule to the Act contains a list of circumstances in which statements will be protected by the defence of qualified privilege. Section 15 of the Act provides that qualified privilege attaches to publication of the reports set out in Pts I and II of the Schedule to the Act, unless the publication is shown to have been made with malice. In Pt I of the Schedule are listed publication of which is protected without the requirement to publish an explanation or contradiction; in Pt II are listed the circumstances in which statements are protected subject to publication of an explanation or contradiction if requested.

Procedural changes

Limitation

Section 5 of the Act reduces the limitation period in which proceedings can be issued for actions for defamation or malicious falsehood from three years to one year. It does not, however, exclude the exercise of the court's discretion. In *Gilberthorpe v News Group Newspapers* (1989) 139 New LJ 1039 a successful application in 1993 by the defendants to strike out for want of prosecution an action which had started in 1987 was overturned by the Court of Appeal in 1995, *inter alia*, on the evidence by the plaintiff that he had been short of funds and in ill-health. (See also Section II, Chapter 7.)

Fast track

A potentially far-reaching reform to the law of libel is contained in the procedural provisions under ss 8–10, the so-called fast track procedure. This gives, for the first time, the right for a plaintiff to apply to the court to have the matter dealt with summarily by a judge alone. The provision under s 8 includes the provision that the judge can dismiss the claim altogether or grant summary relief under s 9. This includes:

(a) a declaration that the statement was defamatory of the plaintiff;
(b) an order that the defendants publish a suitable correction and apology;
(c) an award of damages up to £10,000; and
(d) an order restraining further publication of the libel.

Section 10 contains the appropriate rules regarding the summary procedure, including authorising the court to order the preparation of witness statements by affidavit if necessary.

During the Bill's passage in the House of Commons, there was discussion of increasing the limit for damages from £10,000 to £25,000; but s 9 limits the damages which can be awarded to £10,000. Obviously this fast track procedure will avoid the necessity for an expensive trial and could be particularly appropriate for items in local newspapers or on local radio. However, there is concern among practitioners that the fast track procedure could become overlaid with complexities of providing evidence at a very early stage of the proceedings to prevent a strike-out application since s 8 provides that the court may give judgment for the plaintiff if 'there is no defence to the claim which has a realistic prospect of success'.

Evidential changes

The Act includes three major evidential changes relating to meaning, civil evidence and waiver of proceedings in Parliament.

Meaning

Section 7 provides that the court will no longer be asked to rule on whether a statement is arguably capable as opposed to capable of bearing a particular meaning or meanings attributed to it. This should undoubtedly have the effect of removing a considerable source of expensive interlocutory proceedings.

Conviction

Section 12 of the Act provides that proof that a plaintiff has been convicted of a criminal offence is conclusive evidence that he committed that offence. This provision does not apply to witnesses or defendants. The section itself is an amendment to s 13 of the Civil Evidence Act 1968.

Evidence concerning proceedings in Parliament under s 13 of the Defamation Act 1996

This is a provision that where the conduct of the person in relation to proceedings in Parliament is in issue in defamation proceedings he may waive for the purposes of his proceedings so far as it concerns him the protection of the rule of law which prevents proceedings in Parliament being questioned outside Parliament. This so-called Hamilton amendment will prevent the injustice caused by the actions brought by MPs Neil Hamilton and Rupert Allason against the *Guardian* and *Today* newspapers. Both actions were stayed (see Section II, Chapter 5) but as a result of s 13, both MPs will be able to waive privilege, in relation to themselves only, to enable them to pursue the proceedings and similarly the newspapers will be able to prepare defences.

As has been seen, the action by Neil Hamilton MP was revived but abandoned the day before the trial by the plaintiff and settled on terms which included a modest contribution to the costs of the *Guardian* newspaper. Following the announcement that Neil Hamilton MP was to be investigated by the Parliamentary Commissioner for Standards, the Labour Party has announced that it will seek the repeal of s 13.

The Act does not contain any provision for extending legal aid for libel although the fact that there is no legal aid can be taken into account (see 'Procedural changes' above).

Example

In *Gilberthorpe v News Group Newspapers,* above, the defendants sought to have the plaintiff's action struck out for want of prosecution because there had been a delay of over seven years since the original article was published (see 'Procedural changes' above). The plaintiff stated that the reason for the delay was that he was short of funds and the judge said that lack of legal aid for libel 'should elicit a sympathetic approach from a judge considering an application to strike out on the grounds of delay'.

Neither does the Act contain any provision removing the award of libel damages from the jury to the judge to bring it into line with criminal trials where the jury decides whether or not the accused is guilty but the judge awards the sentence.

Europe

Libel is no exception to the increasing encroachment of European law decisions in all areas of domestic litigation. The European Court has recently given a significant ruling in relation to damages, and has also considered the question of forum for bringing libel actions.

Damages

The European Court of Human Rights in Strasbourg has ruled that the record libel award of £1.5m damages that Count Tolstoy was ordered to pay in 1989 to Lord Aldington was 'disproportionate to the harm suffered' (see Section III, Chapter 9). It further held that both the size of the award and the lack of 'adequate and effective safeguards' against such an award, breached art X of the European Convention of Human Rights guaranteeing freedom of expression. The European Court pointed out that the sum was three times the size of the highest libel award previously in England and it particularly mentioned the fact that there was a failure to insist on any principle of 'proportionality' matching the award of damages to reputation.

The libel, of course, was extremely serious but was contained in a pamphlet, 10,000 copies of which were distributed in the area in which Lord Aldington lived and worked and to MPs (the effect of the action was, of course, as so often happens, to make the alleged libel front-page news for the length of the six-week trial). It would have been open to

Count Tolstoy to have appealed the award in the UK, but he was prevented from doing so because he was not able to lodge the required sum ordered by way of security for Lord Aldington's costs.

This far-reaching decision in relation to what is inherently the domestic law of libel must mean that it is now an option to either party, if the award of libel damages is substantial, to make an application to the European Court of Human Rights, although it is an expensive and exceedingly slow procedure. However, it is important to note that not only was Count Tolstoy not able to go to the Court of Appeal but the matter was taken to the European Court before the Courts and Legal Services Act 1990 was passed (see below).

Forum

The European Court of Human Rights has also given a ruling deciding which was the *forum conveniens* in relation to proceedings for libel. This ruling covers those situations where the alleged libel has been published in several different countries and the plaintiff may be 'forum shopping' to find a preferred country in which to sue.

Example

In *Shevill v Presse-Alliance SA* [1992] 1 All ER 409, an English woman working in Paris was allegedly libelled by the French newspaper *France-Soir*. This had a substantial circulation in France but only some 250 copies in the UK and five in the area the plaintiff lived. She sought to bring libel proceedings in the UK. It was held that it would be open to her to bring proceedings in whichever country she felt her reputation had been damaged. However, if she chose, for example, to bring proceedings in France she would have to abide by the libel laws of that country which might differ to those in the UK, for example, in relation to the presumption of damages.

This is in contrast to *Cumming v Scottish Daily Record, Mail and Sunday Mail Ltd* (1995) *The Times*, 8 June where it was held that the court had jurisdiction to stay proceedings on the grounds of *forum non conveniens* where proceedings had been issued by the plaintiff in one of the jurisdictions in the UK. The plaintiff was Scottish, although he had lived for a short time in England and hoped to work there. He claimed that he had been libelled in an article which was published in the *Sunday Mail* with 850,000 copies published per week, of which about 60,000 were circulated in England. He sought to claim damages in both England and Scotland and the defendant successfully obtained a stay of the English proceedings on the grounds that Scotland was the appropriate forum.

A further contrast can be found in *Pillai v Sarker* (1994) *The Times*, 21 July. In that case the alleged libel was contained in an English language periodical which had a circulation of 73,000 in India and 15 in England. One of the defendants sought to have a writ which had been served on him for damages for libel in this country set aside. The judge held that England was not the natural forum for the issues in the case and that Calcutta was clearly and distinctly the more appropriate forum; this would apply even if the plaintiff continued his claim for damages for injury suffered in England. If followed, this could significantly affect the number of actions where substantial damages are awarded in this country even though the circulation of the alleged libel here is extremely limited. For example, in *Packard v Eleftherotypia* (1987), unreported Commander Packard was awarded what were then record damages of £450,000 for a serious libel in a Greek magazine of which only 87 copies were circulated in the UK.

In relation to security for costs, a foreign company, ordinarily resident in a member state of the European Union, is in no different a situation from an English company. In *Chequepoint SARL v McClelland* (1996) *The Times*, 18 June (see Section II, Chapter 7), an application for security for costs against a foreign plaintiff company was resisted on the grounds that the company was ordinarily resident in a member state of the European Community. It was held, however, that the normal rule should apply, and that security for costs could be awarded in such circumstances.

Internet

The Defamation Act 1996 includes in s 1 a defence providing in effect that only the person responsible for putting the information onto the Internet can be sued. One of the first defamation cases over an alleged defamatory entry on the Internet Worldwide Computer System was recently brought in Australia. The case was undefended but damages of AUS$40,000 were awarded for a statement on the World Wide Bulletin which the plaintiff claimed was defamatory of him. In August 1994, Dr Godfrey, a nuclear physicist, issued a writ in Switzerland claiming damages for libel or slander published on the Internet against a researcher, Dr Philip Hallam-Baker, at the European Swiss Nuclear Physics Laboratory. He claimed that comments about his professional work on Usenet, part of the Internet network used by approximately 16 million people, were defamatory of him. The matter was later settled.

A world precedent was established in April 1996 when a UK firm of solicitors obtained leave to serve proceedings by electronic mail. In the case, an order was sought to restrain a defendant in Europe from publishing alleged defamatory material about a client on the Internet. The only available address was the defendant's e-mail address and the writ, affidavit and the *ex parte* order were served to the defendant's e-mail address. Receipt of the order was confirmed because a returned receipt facility of the e-mail confirmed delivery.

There are interesting problems, as yet unresolved in relation to the Internet, not only whether it is libel or slander, but the question of who is responsible for authorising its repetition beyond the person originally entering the material into the system. The most recently decided cases in America appear to conflict.

Example

In *Cubby Inc v Compuserve Inc* 776 F Supp 135 ((1991) SD NY) where the on-line service provider had delegated editorial control to a third party, the defendant, Compuserve, was exonerated on the basis that 'it had no more control in fact over the content than any other secondary distributor'. This is to be contrasted with the case of *Stratton Oakmont Inc v Prodegy Services Company* (1995) NY MISC Lexis 229 where the defendant was found to have been a publisher because it had taken editorial control.

In 1996, Hammer Distribution issued a writ for libel against Martin Orpen over an alleged libel in an information broadcast on the Internet. Unlike some Internet actions, this action appears to be against the person who had placed the statement on the Internet. Employers certainly could be liable for defamation e-mails sent by their employees.

Appeal

As in any civil litigation, it is open to either party to appeal against a decision if there exist the grounds for appeal. The vast majority of libel cases are decided in favour of the plaintiff, so the majority of appeals are lodged by defendants against quantum of damages and occasionally on liability. In *Walker and Wingsail v Yachting World* (1994), unreported, appeals on liability and quantum were lodged, but as frequently happens, the matter was settled shortly before the appeal was due to be heard.

As can be seen by the chart in Appendix D showing the highest and lowest libel damges award, the level of damages awarded in years 1986 to 1996 by juries in recent years continues to vary widely. It seems wholly wrong that a defendant should have to include in his estimate of the costs of defending an action, the likely costs of taking the matter to appeal. Although the Defamation Act 1996 does not remove the award of damages from the jury and place it with the judge, which would undoubtedly both lower the damages and make them more consistent, there are three factors which should have the effect of reducing and stabilising the lottery which libel damages, at the date of writing, remain. The three factors are:

(a) the Courts and Legal Services Act 1990, s 8;
(b) the Court of Appeal Elton John Guidelines 1995; and
(c) the European Court of Human Rights' decision in *Tolstoy* in the UK 1995.

Courts and Legal Services Act 1990, s 8

This section for the first time gave the Court of Appeal power to substitute for the sum awarded by a jury, such sum as the court thought proper rather than remitting the case back to a jury to reconsider the question of damages. It was hoped that this provision would be widely used and would form a body of decisions which would stabilise damages. However, there have only been four cases under s 8. These are covered below.

Examples

In July 1991 Teresa Gorman was awarded £150,000 against her constituency Chairman Anthony Mudd. On appeal under s 8, this was reduced to £50,000 in October 1992.

In December 1991, Esther Rantzen was awarded £250,000 damages against the *People* newspaper. On appeal under s 8, this was reduced in March 1993 to £110,000. Interestingly, the appeal under that section also referred to art X of the European Convention on Human Rights, and in reducing the award the court recognised its importance.

In October 1991, Dr Smith was awarded £150,000 damages against his partner, Dr Houston, in a slander action where the alleged slander had been published to only a few people in a waiting room. This was reduced on appeal under s 8 in December 1993 to £50,000.

The fourth appeal under s 8 was Elton John against the *Sunday Mirror* in 1995. In November 1993, Elton John was awarded £275,000 punitive damages and £75,000 compensatory damages against the *Sunday Mirror*. On the appeal under s 8, the punitive damages were reduced to £50,000 and the compensatory damages to £25,000. It was in this case that the Guidelines were set out (see Section III, Chapter 9).

While s 8 has clearly not been used sufficiently since its introduction to induce a standard levelling off, two recent settlements shortly before appeal would indicate that plaintiffs are recognising that awards are likely to be reduced on appeal. In June 1995, the football manager, Graeme Souness, was awarded £750,000 damages against the *People* newspaper for an article which had criticised his behaviour toward his ex-wife over their divorce. Shortly before the appeal was due to be heard in November 1995, he agreed to accept £100,000 damages. He had to repay £150,000 to the *People* since he had been paid £250,000 at the end of the trial, the rest having been frozen. In the second case, the award of record damages of £1,485,000 to Mr and Mrs Walker and their company, Wingsail, against *Yachting World* magazine in July 1994 was also settled very shortly before the appeal on the basis of agreed damages to all three plaintiffs of £160,000.

Court of Appeal Elton John Guidelines 1995

In a far-reaching judgment at the hearing of the s 8 appeal in the Elton John case, the Master of the Rolls laid down specific guidelines designed to assuage the public's concern that libel damages were considerably out of line when compared to those for personal injury. The judgment itself is a masterly review of the history of damages which commented:

> It is in our view offensive to public opinion, and rightly so, that a defamation plaintiff should recover damages for injury to reputation greater, perhaps by a significant factor, than if that same plaintiff had been rendered a helpless cripple or an insensate vegetable. The time has in our view come when judges, and counsel, should be free to draw the attention of juries to these comparisons.

The judgment concluded by recommending that juries should be given a tariff of comparisons with personal injury awards such as awards for loss of limb, £52,000; loss of sight, £90,000 and quadriplegia, £125,000.

The judgment was generally welcomed by practitioners and was referred to in two cases shortly afterwards (see Section III, Chapter 9). The MP, Peter Bottomley, had sued Express Newspapers and was awarded £40,000; his fellow MP, David Ashby, had sued the *Sunday Times* but lost. In January 1996, two police officers sued the BBC and although a bracket of proposed damages were put to the jury, in fact they were awarded less than the brackets given by counsel, PC Wright being awarded £12,500 and PC Callaghan £4,000. However, there was concern that the application of the guidelines might vary between judges. In the case of the surgeon, Mr Percy, who sued Mirror Group Newspapers over three articles in February 1996, only two months after the guidelines, these were not applied and an award of £625,000 was made. The matter was settled for £120,000 shortly before appeal. (See Section III, Chapter 9.)

European Court of Human Rights

The decision of the European Court of Human Rights that the award of record damages to Lord Aldington, infringed Count Tolstoy's rights under art X of the European Convention on Human Rights means that there may be a long stop in Europe to prevent excessive awards.

Chapter 12

General Advice

This Chapter examines some of the tactics and general considerations which must apply to either side involved in a libel action.

Set out in Appendix A is a list of reported libel awards for 1986–1996. These show, firstly, that very few cases are lost by a plaintiff: in the last ten years there have only been approximately 20 cases where the plaintiff has either lost his action or abandoned it. The second matter which emerges from this list is the wide variation in damages. While the effect of the new appeals procedure and guidelines is starting to be felt, it is still difficult to give a realistic estimate to a plaintiff or defendant as to the likely amount of any award. As stated above, the extent of the circulation of the alleged libel does not always appear to be taken into account and very often, in the case of tabloid newspapers, there appears to be an element of wishing to punish the newspaper, perhaps for intrusive or unwarranted behaviour, rather than for compensating the plaintiff for any damage to his reputation.

The expense of High Court litigation is such that both parties need to consider very carefully the economics of continuing such proceedings, when the cost of a two to three week trial can amount to £500,000.

Example
In a recent case Ian Hill of Bristol Uniforms successfully defended an action for libel and malicious falsehood brought against him by David Matthews and his company Mattex Ltd in 1992 (*Matthews and Mattex v Hill and British Uniforms* (1995), unreported). The proceedings arose out of statements allegedly made by Mr Hill querying whether Mattex material supplied to fire brigades was of a sufficient quality to protect firemen, together with a video showing the poor performance of a Mattex firesuit. In July 1995, Mr Hill successfully defended the action, and after an 11-day hearing, the case was discontinued by the plaintiff and Mr Hill was awarded his costs. However, a year after the trial he was still

substantially out of pocket because of the complexities of taxing and reimbursing his legal costs.

Arbitration is, of course, an option open to both parties to a libel action. In 1992 Popplewell J brought proceedings for libel against the *Today* newspaper and in the first arbitration of its kind he was awarded £7,500. Alternative dispute resolution is also an option available to both parties which may reduce the costs.

Tactics

This book has sought to cover the basic principles and procedures needed for a libel action to be pursued or defended. In practical terms however, it is important to consider not only the normal risks of litigation, such as whether a witness will stand up to cross-examination, but also whether a plaintiff's objective might be achieved by a settlement. For this purpose without prejudice negotiations, while useful in any litigation, are particularly valuable in libel actions. As mentioned earlier, a prompt payment in at the beginning of the procedure can put pressure on the plaintiff who may thereby have put his costs at risk at an early stage of the action. Discovery can, and frequently is, a make or break point in a libel action. This is also an occasion when the solicitors can meet for inspection of documents so that without prejudice discussions can be initiated informally.

As the trial draws nearer and pressure mounts and the financial consequence of failure looms, a timely offer of a statement in open court can appear attractive to a plaintiff. Similarly, a defendant faced with the likely costs of a trial and, in the case of a newspaper, the possibility that any journalist giving evidence may not be believed, may well find it more attractive to pay an agreed sum, which need not be disclosed to the court, and to join in a statement in open court, rather than face a trial.

As there is no legal aid for libel, occasionally a litigant in person may either bring or defend libel proceedings. The libel action brought by McDonalds, the hamburger chain, against two defendants who are representing themselves began in 1994, and at the time of going to press is still continuing, making it the longest libel action in English legal history. As in any litigation with a plaintiff in person, the court has to be particularly careful to ensure that the plaintiff is aware of his rights, but these can also be exploited. In one particular case a plaintiff in person had been in without prejudice negotiations for some months. Although apparently aware of the full meaning of 'without prejudice', on the first day in court he gave a different impression to the judge and succeeded in having all the without prejudice correspondence including offers by way of damages, placed before the jury. The judge overruled the objections from the defendants.

Another factor which can influence a plaintiff is that a high profile libel action, which is often reported now almost as a form of entertainment, can result in the alleged libel being given a far wider circulation than at the time of the first publication. The most glaring example of this was the action by Gillian Taylforth brought against the *Sun* newspaper in 1994 which was front-page news and a prominent item on television news for the duration of the trial, giving far greater publicity to the alleged libel even than the original publication in the *Sun*. This can be an additional factor in negotiating a settlement on behalf of a defendant.

Costs of litigation are high, libel being no exception (for example, the Botham and Lamb libel action against Imran Khan which lasted two weeks, was estimated to have cost £500,000). A Plaintiff must be made aware that if he is successful and even if he recovers damages and costs, in practice, he will only recover approximately two-thirds of his costs, because of the taxing procedure (see Section III, Chapter 9). This is another reason why a negotiated settlement in which payment of the costs can be agreed before the trial, can be more attractive to the plaintiff. Although he would have to accept a reduced sum by way of damages, he avoids the uncertainty and if the costs are paid in full as part of the settlement, he knows that the sum by way of damages will be paid to him clear of any deductions.

If a plaintiff recovers damages and is awarded costs, then the taxation procedure in which a Taxing Master will decide what proportion of the costs claimed he is entitled to, can last a considerable amount of time. Reference has already been made to the *Mattex* and *Tolstoy* cases. In the *Mattex* case (see p170 above), the successful plaintiff still has not been paid the costs awarded to him a year after the trial; in the *Tolstoy* case, the plaintiff has yet to receive any damages or costs seven years after he was awarded record damages of £1.5m and costs.

Apart from the fast track procedure mentioned earlier, it remains the right of the plaintiff to have a jury. Defendants should bear in mind that for the vast majority of juries, it will be their first experience of a libel case; their only knowledge may be from newspaper reports of substantial damages in high profile cases, whose subsequent successful appeals rarely get reported. As mentioned above, it may take a little time for a levelling in libel damages to occur.

Pre-publication advice

Where it is proposed to publish material which might be defamatory, it is always wise for a client to obtain pre-publication advice. A preliminary decision should be made as to what is likely to be defamatory, and the author, journalist or broadcaster should then be asked to provide the information to enable advice to be given on defences if a writ for libel is issued in respect of the proposed publication. It should be emphasised that the mere fact that the matter has been published already does not make it true, although it may indicate that the plaintiff is less likely to sue.

Often, with experience, it will be possible to make amendments to the proposed libel which will make publication a fair risk, while where there is no evidence, the matter should be deleted. In cases where there is serious defamation, for which there is evidence of justification, it is prudent to obtain signed statements, if possible, before publication. This means that if there is an *ex parte* application for an interlocutory injunction the evidence is immediately available to file an affidavit stating that the defence will be justification. This should result in the injunction being lifted if it has already been granted *ex parte*, or refused if the application is on notice.

It is also the case that when giving pre-publication advice it is advisable to delete some of the defamatory material so that if the plaintiff should institute proceedings he can be made aware that the published material is the tip of the iceberg, and that if the matter goes to trial more allegations will be ventilated. Needless to say this is a policy which should not be adopted unless there is clear evidence of justification in relation to all the defamatory statements, whether or not they have been published.

It is never possible to say that a writ will not be issued, since a plaintiff may have many reasons for issuing proceedings, for example, the late Robert Maxwell was a master of the gagging writ. Lord Woolf, in his 'Access to Justice Report', is preparing sweeping changes to civil litigation which will result in the control of civil proceedings being given to the court. This will make it harder for a plaintiff to issue a writ and then not pursue the matter. However, it must always be assumed that those rich and powerful enough will continue to attempt to prevent publication of matters to which they object. Some public relations companies are now very assiduous in their attempts on behalf of their clients to prevent publication of matters to which a client objects, even if the statements can be justified.

Particular care needs to be taken where the plaintiff is either rich or is funded. For example, a number of police officers have had considerable success in bringing proceedings for libel in recent years because they are backed by the Police Federation; similarly, trade union or representative bodies will often fund a member plaintiff's libel action. In the same way regard needs to be had to the potential defendants. If they are a large multi-national with deep pockets, they may protract the proceedings, perhaps make a number of expensive interlocutory applications, which an individual plaintiff may find intimidating, and generally exploit their strength. However, under the civil justice reforms proposed by Lord Woolf, if the conduct of litigation is passed to the control of the court, then delaying tactics will not be open to a defendant. Similarly, a plaintiff will not be able to issue a gagging writ and take no further action.

Speed

Lawyers are frequently criticised for being slow but libel is a branch of the law where speed is of the essence for both parties. For a plaintiff who has been libelled, it is essential that he take immediate steps to prevent repetition and/or to obtain an apology and correction as soon as possible and otherwise try to limit the damage to his reputation. For a defendant and his advisors, it is essential that all steps must be taken immediately a claim has been received to ascertain whether there is any evidence to support a substantive defence. If not, a decision must be taken quickly as to whether to offer an apology as part of a settlement or run a unilateral apology and plead that in mitigation, or make a payment in or withdraw the publication, or otherwise limit the potential claim.

In a number of cases in recent years, where very substantial damages have been awarded against newspapers, the plaintiff has frequently said 'if I had been offered an apology early in the proceedings, I would have been content with that.' It is also the fact that juries can be influenced by the fact that no apology has been offered, particularly where the defendants are not able to put a substantive defence together at trial. The prominence of an apology is also a matter for consideration. If the original story was a front-page headline it can be counter-productive to publish an apology at the bottom of page 13 or for that matter to couch it in grudging terms.

The advantage to a defendant of investigating thoroughly after a letter before action is that occasionally information is obtained which significantly adds to the information which was available before publication of the alleged libel. In three cases where the author was asked to give advice after publication of the alleged libel, investigations enabled an extremely detailed and strong rebuttal to the letter before action to be sent. One claim arose out of allegations of impropriety by the plaintiff in relation to claiming expenses on a film. Inquiries revealed that the claimant not only had convictions for fraud but was masquerading under a false name. A detailed response outlining these facts were sent to his solicitor, who clearly had not been informed of all the facts, and no further word was heard. In another case a senior figure in the insurance world claimed to have an income of a certain amount and detailed inquiries from a number of different companies with which he was associated showed his income to be well in excess of his claimed income. The letter played the decisive part in the disposing of the action on reasonable terms. Finally a case involving a plc accused of irregular accounting practices was settled with no payment as to damages because of inquiries made after publication uncovered far more serious accounting irregularities than those set out in the newspaper article complained of.

Defamation is an absorbing and important branch of the law and in the days of worldwide instant communication of continuing relevance. The basic principles and balances which govern the opposing requirements of free speech and a free press on the one hand, against a need to protect reputation on the other hand, are vital in an era of rapid global communication.

A legitimate criticism of libel proceedings is the expense and length of trial but the new fast track procedure should be beneficial in this regard in enabling people of modest means to protect their reputation in the absence of legal aid. Similarly, the provisions for exchange of witness statements and rulings on meaning at an early stage of the proceedings should reduce the length of those actions which do come to trial.

In this author's view, the Defamation Act 1996 has made a number of improvements to the practice and procedure in defamation proceedings which are likely to reduce costs, time and simplify the procedures. However, it is regretted that the opportunity was not taken to take the responsibility for awarding damages away from the jury. It is vital that the jury should be retained because of the basic principle set out in the Magna Carta that where a man's life or reputation is at stake, he should be entitled to be judged by a jury of his peers. However, as in criminal trials, the practice that the jury pronounce a verdict and the judge decides the sentence, could be more appropriate. In libel trials this would mean that the jury would be retained to find out whether or not the words were defamatory, but it would be left to the judge to decide the award of damages.

The price of freedom is eternal vigilance and the defamation law is no exception. There will always be those that wish to stifle any form of criticism. At the same time, there are those who may have their own motives in making unjustified attacks on the reputation of others. Both situations require that a remedy exists in law.

Appendix A

Libel Awards July 1986 to August 1996

July 1986	Marcie-Riviere v Taki Theodoracopulos	£15,000
July 1986	Ormston v North East Broadcasting	£8,250
Nov 1986	Maxwell v Pressdram (£50,000 exemplary damages)	£55,000
Mar 1987	Countess of Dudley v Literary Review	£5,000
June 1987	Packard v Eleftherotypia	£450,000
July 1987	Jeffrey Archer v Daily Star	£500,000
Nov 1987	Sethia v Mail on Sunday (reduced by agreement later)	£260,000
Feb 1988	C Freeman v Stationery Trade News	£300,000
May 1988	Gilberthorpe v Daily Mirror	£9,750
May 1988	Gilberthorpe v The Sun	£28,750
June 1988	Michael Meacher v Observer	Lost
July 1988	Fox and Gibbons v Sourakia	£310,000
July 1988	Kiffin v Mail on Sunday	£9,000
July 1988	Ellis-Carr v Mail on Sunday	£14,000
July 1988	Mcnally v Evening Standard	£140,000
July 1988	Murphy v Sunday Telegraph	£10,000
	Hamilton and Howarth v BBC (settlement)	£50,000
Oct 1988	Koo Stark v Sunday People	£300,000
Oct 1988	Sethia v Hindustani Times	£40,000
Oct 1988	McCartney and Boal v Sunday World	£100,000
Oct 1988	Scruton v Observer	£75,000
Nov 1988	Johnson v Radio City	£350,000
Dec 1988	Elton John v The Sun (settlement of 17 libel actions)	£1,000,000
Jan 1989	Maureen Smith v Express Newspapers	£5,000
Jan 1989	Gross v Goodman	£3,000
Mar 1989	Anne Chastell and Frances Warby v Tesco (payment in £1,500 each)	£800 each (Increased on appeal to £7,500 each)
May 1989	Kevin Maddocks v Angling Times	£150,000

May 1989	Sonia Sutcliffe v Private Eye	£600,000
May 1989	Masters v Mirror Group Newspapers	£65,000
June 1989	Bates v Harris	£71,500
June 1989	Smith and Holland v Mirror Group Newspapers	£90,000
July 1989	Tobias v Mail on Sunday	£470,000
Oct 1989	Kit Miller v Daily Mirror/People	£165,000
Oct 1989	Chastell and Warby v Tesco (£7,500 each on appeal)	£15,000
Nov 1989	Wadsworth v Freud	£10,000
Nov 1989	Mackeson v Willis	1p
Nov 1989	Aldington v Tolstoy and Watts	£1,500,000
Dec 1989	Professor Hartt v Independent (payment in £5,000) (judge alone)	£7,500
Dec 1989	Trebith v Sunday Sport (payment in £60,500)	£60,000
Dec 1989	Clay v Mirror Group (payment in £10,000)	£7,500
1989	Abunamous v Nakhle	£15,000
Nov 1989	Mardas v Mirror	£75,000
Jan 1990	Carroll v Times	£4,000
Jan 1990	Neil and Sunday Times v Peregrine Worsthorne	£1,000
	2nd pl	60p
Feb 1990	Ken Bates v Daily Mirror	£2,500
Feb 1990	Noah v Shuba	£7,500
Mar 1990	Tessa Sanderson v Mirror Group Newspapers	£30,000
Mar 1990	Murphy and Murphy v Times Newspapers	£15,000(Ir)
Mar 1990	Lord Linley v Today (£30,000 exemplary damages)	£35,000
	Sam Klibansky v Ha Olam Hazeh (judge alone)	£100,000
May 1990	Zahida Seemi v Sadiq (slander)	£20,000
May 1990	Duncan Campbell v BBC (settlement)	£50,000
June 1990	Lim v News of The World	Lost
June 1990	Slipper v BBC (settlement)	£50,000
June 1990	Grudzinskas v Mirror	£25,000
June 1990	Frank Warren v Daily Mirror	£10,000
July 1990	Gaynor Winyard and Another v Tatler (mother £75,000 and son £15,000)	£90,000
July 1990	Ranulph Twistleton-Fiennes v Mackans (reduced after notice of appeal lodged)	£100,000
Oct 1990	David Prendergast v NUM	£100,000
Oct 1990	David Morrel v Construction News	£101,000
Oct 1990	Winter v News Scotland Ltd	£50,000
Nov 1990	PC Nurtherm v Mirror Group Newspapers	£25,000
Nov 1990	Sedgemore v Kilroy-Silk and The Times	Jury failed to agree. Retrial ordered. Case subsequently abandoned

Nov 1990	Earl of Stradbroke v Gilbey		£40,000
Nov 1990	Shiner v BBC		£25,000
Oct 1990	James Rowland Jones v City & Westminster Financial plc		£130,000
	(exemplary damages £20,000)		
Dec 1990	Sonia Sutcliffe v News of The World		Lost
Jan 1991	Tom O'Connor v The People		abandond
Jan 1991	PC Williams and Baker v The People		Lost
Feb 1991	Siouxie and The Banshees v Daily Mirror		£10,000
	(settlement damages and costs)		
Feb 1991	Golding v Pressdram (payment in £5,000)		£1,500
Mar 1991	Walker, Cartmell and Wickham	1st Pl	£40,000
	Laboratories Ltd v Central TV	2nd Pl	Lost
	(payments in of £2,500, £1,500		
	and £500)	3rd Pl	£5,000
Mar 1991	Proetta v Sunday Times (settlement)		£25,000
Mar 1991	Michael Seaston v Spery (settlement)		£10,000
Apr 1991	Hooper v British Airways		£10,000
	(settlement damages and costs)		
Apr 1991	Gavin Campbell v Today (settlement)		£15,000
May 1991	Currie v Observer		£5,000
May 1991	Bachchan v India Abroad		£40,000
May 1991	Honeyford v Commission for Racial Equality		£20,000
	(settlement)		
May 1991	Jonathan Hunt (6) and Mrs Hunt v Sun		
	(settlement)		£35,000
May 1991	David Bookbinder v Norman Tebbit		Lost
June 1991	Welsh v TGWU		£130,000
June 1991	Lim v News of The World		Appeal dismissed
June 1991	Macloughlin v News Group (majority verdict)		£50,000
July 1991	Christopher Geidt and Anthony De Norman v Central TV (settlement)		£100,000 each
July 1991	Teresa Gorman v Anthony Mudd		£150,000
	(reduced on appeal to £50,000 October 1992)		
Aug 1991	Maurice Lubin v HTV (no order for costs)		£1
Aug 1991	Prodev Ltd v HTV		Lost
Oct 1991	Smith v Houston (slander) (reduced on appeal to £50,000 Dec 1993)		£150,000
Oct 1991	Anthony Pargeter v The Sport		£40,000
Oct 1991	Jennifer Robert Noble v Gordon and		
	Penelope Steel (libel and slander)	1st Pl	£15,750
		2nd Pl	£9,975
Nov 1991	Roache v The Sun (payment in £50,000)		£50,000
	(costs from payment in awarded		
	to Sun on appeal November 1992)		

Nov 1991	Gunasekera v Samco Agencies	£150,000
Nov 1991	Standish v The People (majority decision)	Finding for plaintiff but no damages
Nov 1991	Dusty Springfield v TVS	£75,000
Dec 1991	Esther Rantzen v The People (reduced on appeal to £110,000 March 1993)	£250,000
Jan 1992	Jason Connery v The Sun	£35,000
Jan 1992	WPC Robson v Nigel Flood (settlement)	£500
Jan 1992	Laura Watson v Arglers & Court (slander) (judge alone)	Lost
Feb 1992	PC Robert Taylor v Chapman (judge alone)	£2,500
Feb 1992	Sara Keays v New Woman	£105,000
Feb 1992	Spittle v Hughes	£20,000
Mar 1992	Vladimir Telnikoff v Vladimir Matusevich (second trial) (appeal lodged)	£240,000
Mar 1992	Barney Eastwood v Barry McGuigan (in Northern Ireland)	£450,000
Apr 1992	Jason Donovan v Face	£200,000
Apr 1992	Faragy v Al-Hayat	£170,000
May 1992	Duncan Campbell v The Pink Paper	£20,000
May 1992	Wafic Said v Misbah Baki	£400,000
June 1992	Peter Clarke v Newspaper Publishing	£20,000
June 1992	Irving Scholar v Daily Mail	£100,000
July 1992	Robertson v Sunday Express (settlement)	£50,000
July 1992	Judge Popplewell v Today (arbitration)	£7,500
July 1992	Dixons v Thames TV (£5,000 in court)	£1
July 1992	Antony Gecas v Scottish Television (Scotland)	Lost
Aug 1992	Jani Allen v Channel Four Television	Lost
Sept 1992	Mona Bauwens v The People	Jury failed to agree. Retrial ordered
Oct 1992	Teresa Gorman v Mudd (s 8 appeal) (July 91 award of £150,000 reduced on appeal)	£50,000
Oct 1992	Frank Warren v Terry Marsh	Lost
Oct 1992	Sean Hannan v Thames TV	£5,000
Nov 1992	Mitch Mitchell v Book Sales Ltd	Lost
Nov 1992	Rupert Allason v Daily Mirror (settlement damages and costs)	£225,000
Nov 1992	Bill Roache v The Sun (appeal re: costs after Nov 1991 Award)	Costs to Defendants from date of payment in.
Dec 1992	Peter Martyn v B Railways (slander)	£50,000

Dec 1992	George Galloway MP v Daily Mirror and Daily Record		£150,000
Jan 1993	Richard Branson and Virgin Atlantic v British Airways	1st Pl	£500,000
	(Settlement)	2nd Pl	£110,000
Feb 1993	Derbyshire County Council v Times Newspapers Ltd		Lost
Mar 1993	Esther Rantzen v The People (s 8 appeal) (Dec 1991 award of £250,000 reduced on appeal)		£110,000
May 1993	Dr Paul MacLouglin v Dr Gordon Kells		£85,000
May 1993	Cpl Brian Cooper v Central Independent Television and Cook (settlement)		£100,000
May 1993	Latimer v Scallywag (settlement)		Settled no damages
June 1993	Crown Eyeglass v Associated Newspapers		£7,000
	Joe Lee v Associated Newspapers		£14,000
	Harold Sternfield v Associated Newspapers		£14,000
July 1993	Nigel Bowden v Channel Four (payment in accepted)		£25,050
July 1993	Anita Roddick		£1,000
	Gordon Roddick		£1,000
	The Body Shop v Channel Four		£1,000
		Special damages	£273,000
July 1993	St Steve Turnbull v Shooting News		£2,000
July 1993	John Major and Clare Latimer v New Statesman (settlement)		£1,001 each
Aug 1993	Julia Charlton v Streetlife (settlement)		£75,000
Sept 1993	Joyce v Sengupta and Today (malicious falsehood)		£25,000
Nov 1993	Elton John v Mirror Group Newspapers (£275,000 punitive damages £75,000 damages)		£350,000
Nov 1993	Sarfraz Nawaz v Allan Lamb		Abandoned
Nov 1993	McCarthy and Stone v Daily Telegraph		Abandoned
Dec 1993	Smith v Houston (slander) (s 8 appeal) Oct 91 award of £150,000 reduced on appeal)		£50,000
Jan 1994	Major v Scallywag (settlement)		No damages
Jan 1994	Taylforth v The Sun (majority verdict 10-2)		Lost
April 1994	Buckingham v Dove and Rusk		Lost
May 1994	Halpin v Oxford Polytechnic and Professor Trevor Watkin		£65,000
May 1994	Upjohn v BBC		£60,000
	The Upjohn Company and Upjohn Ltd v BBC		£25,000
June 1994	Gregg Harris v John Patten		Settled

June 1994	Wraith v Wraith (slander)	£69
	(each side to pay its own costs)	
July 1994	John Walker	£450,000
	Jean Walker	£35,000
	Walker Wingsail Systems v Yachting World,	
	Andrew Bray and IPC Magazines	£1,000,000
July 1994	Law For All v Coventry Evening Telegraph	£6,000
Dec 1994	Anglesea v Independent on Sunday (settlement)	£107,000
	Observer	£80,000
	Private Eye	£80,000
	HTV	£107,000
Jan 1995	Paul Judge v Guardian	Lost
Feb 1995	Jones v Mirror Group Newspapers	£115,000
	(£100,000 general damages,	
	£15,000 special damages)	
Feb 1995	Erokhina v MGN	£60,000
	(liability admitted; trial on quantum)	
Feb 1995	Harris v Lodge	settlement
April 1995	Dr Giwa-Osagie v Hall and Smithson	£45,000
April 1995	PC Eggleton v Asda (e-mail)	settlement
May 1995	Brasher and Disley v Channel Four (settlement)	£380,000
June 1995	Graeme Souness v Daily Mirror	£750,000
July 1995	Matthews and Mattex v Hill & Bristol Uniforms	Abandoned
July 1995	Dr Chohan v Oxford University Press	1p
July 1995	Newton v New World	£15,000
July 1995	Ward v Kingston	£1,000
July 1995	Martyn Gregory v The Government	£40,000
July 1995	Bio Health Ltd v BBC	£100,000
	(settlement damages and costs)	
July 1995	Bennett v Portland Publishing	£15,000
Aug 1995	Hubbard v Committee of Driffield Club	Lost
Aug 1995	Walker and Wingsail v Yachting World	
	(settlement just before appeal) damages	£160,000
Oct 1995	Philip McHugh v News Group	£3,000
Oct 1995	De Freitas v Wisden Cricket Monthly	
	(settlement)	£50,000
Nov 1995	Milner v Terry Osbourne (slander)	£40
Nov 1995	Souness v The People	
	(reduced by agreement before appeal)	£100,000
Nov 1995	Joe Homan v Associated Newspapers Ltd	£30,000
Dec 1995	Halpin v Oxford Polytechnic	Verdict set aside by Court of Appeal. New trial ordered
Dec 1995	Elton John v Mirror Group Newspapers	

	(November 1993 award £275,000 exemplary damages reduced)		£50,000
	(£75,000 compensatory damages reduced)		£25,000
	(Court of Appeal Guidelines)		
Dec 1995	Osagie v Doncaster NHS Hospital Trust		£40,000
Dec 1995	Bottomley v The Sunday Express		£40,000
Dec 1995	Ashby v The Sunday Times		Lost
Jan 1996	Wright and Callaghan v BBC	1st Pl	£12,500
		2nd Pl	£4,000
Feb 1996	Percy v Mirror Group Newspapers (3 articles)		£625,000
Mar 1996	Howarth v Guardian		£15,000
	(settlement during cross-examination of plaintiff statement in open court)		
Apr 1996	Powers v The Sun (settlement damages and costs)		£100,000
Apr 1996	Dolores O'Riordan v The Sport		£5,000
May 1996	Rupert Allason MP v MGN Ltd		Lost
	(malicious falsehood)		
May 1996	McCartan Turkington and Breen v Daily Telegraph (Northern Ireland)		£130,000
	Christie Bourke v Sun and Radio Telefis Eireann (Eire)		£15,000
June 1996	Bookbinder v Sunday Times (settlement damages and costs)		£600,000
July 1996	Dr James Sharp v BBC and New Statesman (malicious falsehood and libel)		Abandoned after 7 days
July 1996	Botham and Lamb v Khan		Lost
July 1996	Dolores O'Riordan v Daily Star (settlement damages and costs)		£10,000
Aug 1996	Doder v Time Magazine (settlement)		£175,000
Sept 1996	Anthony Steen v Mail on Sunday (settlement damages and costs)		£100,000
Oct 1996	Hamilton and Greer v Guardian Newspapers (each plaintiff paid £7,500 to defendants' costs)		Settlement
Oct 1996	Sultan v New Statesman and BBC		Abandoned
Nov 1996	Albert Reynolds v Sunday Times (payment in £5,005)		1p

Appendix B

Defamation Act 1952
Ch 66

An Act to amend the law relating to libel and slander and other malicious false-hoods. [30th October 1952.]

Broadcast statements

1. For the purposes of the law of libel and slander, the broadcasting of words by means of wireless telegraphy shall be treated as publication in permanent form.

Slander affecting official, professional or business reputation

2. In an action for slander in respect of words calculated to disparage the plaintiff in any office, profession, calling, trade or business held or carried on by him at the time of the publication, it shall not be necessary to allege or prove special damage. OP whether or not the words are spoken of the plaintiff in the way of his office, profession, calling, trade or business.

Slander of title, &c

3.—(1) In an action for slander of title, slander of goods or other malicious falsehood. it shall not be necessary to allege or title &c prove special damage—

    (a) if the words upon which the action is founded are calculated to cause pecuniary damage to the plaintiff and are published in writing or other permanent form; or

    (b) if the said words are calculated to cause pecuniary damage to the plaintiff in respect of any office. profession. calling, trade or business held or carried on by him at the time of the publication.

(2) Section one of this Act shall apply for ,the purposes of this section as it applies for the purposes of the law of libel and slander.

Unintentional defamation

4.—(1) A person who has published words alleged to be defamatory of another person may, if he claims that the words were published by him innocently in relation to that other person, make an offer of amends under this section; and in any such case—

    (a) if the offer is accepted by the party aggrieved and is duly performed, no proceedings for libel or slander shall be taken or continued by that party against the person making the offer in respect of the publication in question (but without prejudice to any cause of action against any other person jointly responsible for that publication);

    (b) if the offer is not accepted by the party aggrieved then, except as otherwise provided by this section, it shall be a defence, in any proceedings by him for libel or slander against the person making the offer in respect of the publication in question, to prove that the words complained of were published by the defendant innocently in relation to the plaintiff and that the offer was made as soon as practicable after the defendant received notice that they were or might be defamatory of the plaintiff, and has not been withdrawn.

(2) An offer of amends under this section must be expressed to be made for the purposes of this section, and must be accompanied by an affidavit specifying the facts relied upon by the person making it to show that the words in question were published by him innocently in relation to the party aggrieved; and for the purposes of a defence under paragraph (b) of subsection (1) of this section no evidence, other than evidence of facts specified in the affidavit, shall be admissible on behalf of that person to prove that the words were so published.

(3) An offer of amends under this section shall be understood to mean an offer—

    (a)   in any case, to publish or join in the publication of a suitable correction of the words complained of, and a sufficient apology to the party aggrieved in respect of those words;

    (b)   where copies of a document or record containing the said words have been distributed by or with the knowledge of the person making the offer, to take such steps as are reasonably practicable on his part for notifying persons to whom copies have been so distributed that the words are alleged to be defamatory of the party aggrieved.

(4) Where an offer of amends under this section is accepted by the party aggrieved—

    (a)   any question as to the steps to be taken in fulfilment of the offer as so accepted shall in default of agreement between the parties be referred to and determined by the High Court, whose decision thereon shall be final;

    (b)   the power of the court to make orders as to costs in proceedings by the party aggrieved against the person making the offer in respect of the publication in question, or in proceedings in respect of the offer under paragraph (a) of this subsection, shall include power to order the payment by the person making the offer to the party aggrieved of costs on an indemnity basis and any expenses reasonably incurred or to be incurred by that party in consequence of the publication in question;

and if no such proceedings as aforesaid are taken, the High Court may, upon application made by the party aggrieved, make any such order for the payment of such costs and expenses as aforesaid as could be made in such proceedings.

(5) For the purposes of this section words shall be treated as published by one person (in this subsection referred to as the publisher) innocently in relation to another person if and only if the following conditions are satisfied, that is to say—

    (a)   that the publisher did not intend to publish them of and concerning that other person, and did not know of circumstances by virtue of which they might be understood to refer to him; or

    (b)   that the words were not defamatory on the face of them, and the publisher did not know of circumstances by virtue of which they might be understood to be defamatory of that other person,

and in either case that the publisher exercised all reasonable care in relation to the publication; and any reference in this subsection to the publisher shall be construed as including a reference to any servant or agent of his who was concerned with the contents of the publication.

(6) Paragraph (b) of subsection (1) of this section shall not apply in relation to the publication by any person of words of which he is not the author unless he proves that the words were written by the author without malice.

Justification

5. In an action for libel or slander in respect of words containing two or more distinct charges against the plaintiff, a defence of justification shall not fail by

reason only that the truth of every charge is not proved if the words not proved to be true do not materially injure the plaintiff's reputation having regard to the truth of the remaining charges.

Fair comment

6. In an action for libel or slander in respect of words consisting partly of allegations of fact and partly of expression of opinion, a defence of fair comment shall not fail by reason only that the truth of every allegation of fact is not proved if the expression of opinion is fair comment having regard to such of the facts alleged or referred to in the words complained of as are proved.

Qualified privilege of newspapers

7.—(1) Subject to the provisions of this section, the publication in a newspaper of any such report or other matter as is mentioned in the Schedule to this Act shall be privileged unless the publication is proved to be made with malice.

(2) In an action for libel in respect of the publication of any such report or matter as is mentioned in Part II of the Schedule to this Act, the provisions of this section shall not be a defence if it is proved that the defendant has been requested by the plaintiff to publish in the newspaper in which the original publication was made a reasonable letter or statement by way of explanation or contradiction, and has refused or neglected to do so, or has done so in a manner not adequate or not reasonable having regard to all the circumstances.

(3) Nothing in this section shall be construed as protecting the publication of any matter the publication of which is prohibited by law, or of any matter which is not of public concern and the publication of which is not for the public benefit.

(4) Nothing in this section shall be construed as limiting or abridging any privilege subsisting (otherwise than by virtue of section four of the Law of Libel Amendment Act, 1888) immediately before the commencement of this Act.

(5) In this section the expression 'newspaper' means any paper containing public news or observations thereon, or consisting wholly or mainly of advertisements, which is printed for sale and is published in the United Kingdom either periodically or in parts or numbers at intervals not exceeding thirty-six days.

Extent of Law of Libel Amendment Act, 1888, s 3

8. Section three of the Law of Libel Amendment Act, 1888 (which relates to contemporary reports of proceedings before courts exercising judicial authority) shall apply and apply only to courts exercising judicial authority within the United Kingdom.

Extension of certain defences to broadcasting

9.—(1) Section three of the Parliamentary Papers Act, 1840 (which confers protection in respect of proceedings for printing extracts from or abstracts of parliamentary papers) shall have effect as if the reference to printing included a reference to broadcasting by means of wireless telegraphy.

(2) Section seven of this Act and section three of the Law of Libel Amendment Act, 1888, as amended by this Act shall apply in relation to reports or matters broadcast by means of wireless telegraphy as part of any programme or

service provided by means of a broadcasting station within the United Kingdom, and in relation to any broadcasting by means of wireless telegraphy of any such report or matter, as they apply in relation to reports and matters published in a newspaper and to publication in a newspaper; and subsection (2) of the said section seven shall have effect, in relation to any such broadcasting, as if for the words 'in the newspaper in which' there were substituted the words 'in the manner in which.'

(3) In this section 'broadcasting station' means any station in respect of which a licence granted by the Postmaster General under the enactments relating to wireless telegraphy is in force, being a licence which (by whatever form of words) authorises the use of the station for the purpose of providing broadcasting services for general reception.

Limitation on privilege at elections

10. A defamatory statement published by or on behalf of a candidate in any election to a local government authority or to privilege Parliament shall not be deemed to be published on a privileged occasion on the ground that it is material to a question in issue in the election, whether or not the person by whom it is published is qualified to vote at the election.

Agreements for indemnity

11. An agreement for indemnifying any person against civil Agreements liability for libel in respect of the publication of any matter for shall not be unlawful unless at the time of the publication that person knows that the matter is defamatory, and does not reasonably believe there is a good defence to any action brought upon it.

Evidence of other damages recovered by plaintiff

12. In any action for libel or slander the defendant may give evidence in mitigation of damages that the plaintiff has recovered damages, or has brought actions for damages, for libel or slander in respect of the publication of words to the same effect as the words on which the action is founded or has received or agreed to receive compensation in respect of any such publication.

Consolidation of actions for slander, &c

13. Section five of the Law of Libel Amendment Act, 1888 (which provides for the consolidation, on the application of the defendants, of two or more actions for libel by the same plaintiff) shall apply to actions for slander and to actions for slander of title, slander of goods or other malicious falsehood as it applies to actions for libel; and references in that section to the same, or substantially the same, libel shall be construed accordingly.

Application of Act to Scotland

14. This Act shall apply to Scotland subject to the following Application modifications, that is to say:—

(a) sections one, two, eight and thirteen shall be omitted;
(b) for section three there shall be substituted the following section—

'Actions for verbal injury

> 3. In any action for verbal injury it shall not be necessary for the pursuer to aver or prove special damage if the words on which the action is founded are calculated to cause pecuniary damage to the pursuer.';

(c) subsection (2) of section four shall have effect as if at the end thereof there were added the words 'Nothing in this subsection shall be held to entitle a defender to lead evidence of any fact specified in the declaration unless notice of his intention so to do has been given in the defences.'; and

(d) for any reference to libel, or to libel or slander, there shall be substituted a reference to defamation; the expression 'plaintiff' means pursuer; the expression 'defendant' means defender; for any reference to an affidavit made by any person there shall be substituted a reference to a written declaration signed by that person; for any reference to the High Court there shall be substituted a reference to the Court of Session or, if an action of defamation is depending in the sheriff court in respect of the publication in question, the sheriff; the expression 'costs' means expenses; and for any reference to a defence of justification there shall be substituted a reference to a defence of *veritas*.

Legislative powers of Parliament of Northern Ireland

15. No limitation on the powers of the Parliament of Northern Ireland imposed by the Government of Ireland Act, 1920, shall preclude that Parliament from making laws for purposes similar to the purposes of this Act.

Interpretation

16.—(1) Any reference in this Act to words shall be construed as including a reference to pictures, visual images, gestures and other methods of signifying meaning.

(2) The provisions of Part III of the Schedule to this Act shall have effect for the purposes of the interpretation of that Schedule.

(3) In this Act 'broadcasting by means of wireless telegraphy' means publication for general reception by means of wireless telegraphy within the meaning of the Wireless Telegraphy Act, 1949, and 'broadcast by means of wireless telegraphy' shall be construed accordingly.

(4) Where words broadcast by means of wireless telegraphy are simultaneously transmitted by telegraph as defined by the Telegraph Act, 1863, in accordance with a licence granted by the Postmaster General the provisions of this Act shall apply as if the transmission were broadcasting by means of wireless telegraphy.

Proceedings affected and saving

17.—(1) This Act applies for the purposes of any proceedings begun after the commencement of this Act, whenever the cause of action arose, but does not affect any proceedings begun before the commencement of this Act.

(2) Nothing in this Act affects the law relating to criminal libel.

Short title, commencement, extent and repeals

18.—(1) This Act may be cited as the Defamation Act, 1952, and shall come into operation one month after the passing of this Act.

(2) This Act (except section fifteen) shall not extend to Northern Ireland.

(3) Sections four and six of the Law of Libel Amendment Act, 1888, are hereby repealed.

SCHEDULE

Sections 7, 16

NEWSPAPER STATEMENTS HAVING QUALIFIED PRIVILEGE

PART I

STATEMENTS PRIVILEGED WITHOUT EXPLANATION OR CONTRADICTION

1. A fair and accurate report of any proceedings in public of the legislature of any part of Her Majesty's dominions outside Great Britain.

2. A fair and accurate report of any proceedings in public of an international organisation of which the United Kingdom or Her Majesty's Government in the United Kingdom is a member, or of any international conference to which that government sends a representative.

3. A fair and accurate report of any proceedings in public of an international court.

4. A fair and accurate report of any proceedings before a court exercising jurisdiction throughout any part of Her Majesty's dominions outside the United Kingdom, or of any proceedings before a court-martial held outside the United Kingdom under the Naval Discipline Act, the Army Act or the Air Force Act.

5. A fair and accurate report of any proceedings in public of a body or person appointed to hold a public inquiry by the government or legislature of any part of Her Majesty's dominions outside the United Kingdom.

6. A fair and accurate copy of or extract from any register kept in pursuance of any Act of Parliament which is open to inspection by the public, or of any other document which is required by the law of any part of the United Kingdom to be open to inspection by the public.

7. A notice or advertisement published by or on the authority of any court within the United Kingdom or any judge or officer of such a court.

PART II

STATEMENTS PRIVILEGED SUBJECT TO EXPLANATION OR CONTRADICTION

8. A fair and accurate report of the findings or decision of any of the following associations, or of any committee or governing body thereof, that is to say—

  (a) an association formed in the United Kingdom for the purpose of promoting or encouraging the exercise of or interest in any art, science, religion or learning, and empowered by its constitution to exercise control over or adjudicate upon matters of interest or concern to the association, or the actions or conduct of any persons subject to such control or adjudication;

(b)   an association formed in the United Kingdom for the purpose of promoting or safeguarding the interests of any trade, business, industry or profession, or of the persons carrying on or engaged in any trade, business, industry or profession, and empowered by its constitution to exercise control over or adjudicate upon matters connected with the trade, business, industry or profession, or the actions or conduct of those persons;

(c)   an association formed in the United Kingdom for the purpose of promoting or safeguarding the interests of any game, sport or pastime to the playing or exercise of which members of the public are invited or admitted, and empowered by its constitution to exercise control over or adjudicate upon persons connected with or taking part in the game, sport or pastime,

being a finding or decision relating to a person who is a member of or is subject by virtue of any contract to the control of the association.

9. A fair and accurate report of the proceedings at any public meeting held in the United Kingdom, that is to say, a meeting bona fide and lawfully held for a lawful purpose and for the furtherance or discussion of any matter of public concern, whether the admission to the meeting is general or restricted.

10. A fair and accurate report of the proceedings at any meeting or sitting in any part of the United Kingdom of—

(a)   any local authority or committee of a local authority or local authorities;

(b)   any justice or justices of the peace acting otherwise than as a court exercising judicial authority;

(c)   any commission, tribunal, committee or person appointed for the purposes of any inquiry by Act of Parliament, by Her Majesty or by a Minister of the Crown;

(d)   any person appointed by a local authority to hold a local inquiry in pursuance of any Act of Parliament;

(e)   any other tribunal, board, committee or body constituted by or under, and exercising functions under, an Act of Parliament,

not being a meeting or sitting admission to which is denied to representatives of newspapers and other members of the public.

11. A fair and accurate report of the proceedings at a general meeting of any company or association constituted, registered or certified by or under any Act of Parliament or incorporated by Royal Charter, not being a private company within the meaning of the Companies Act, 1948.

12. A copy or fair and accurate report or summary of any notice or other matter issued for the information of the public by or on behalf of any government department, officer of state, local authority or chief officer of police.

PART III

INTERPRETATION

13. In this Schedule the following expressions have the meanings hereby respectively assigned to them, that is to say:—

'Act of Parliament' includes an Act of the Parliament of Northern Ireland, and the reference to the Companies Act, 1948, includes a reference to any corresponding enactment of the Parliament of Northern Ireland;

'government department 'includes a department of the Government of Northern Ireland;

'international court' means the International Court of Justice and any other judicial or arbitral tribunal deciding matters in dispute between States;

'legislature'. in relation to any territory comprised in Her Majesty's dominions which is subject to a central and a local legislature, means either of those legislatures;

'local authority' means any authority or body to which the Local Authorities (Admission of the Press to Meetings) Act, 1908, or the Local Government (Ireland) Act, 1902, as amended by any enactment of the Parliament of Northern Ireland, applies;

'part of Her Majesty's dominions' means the whole of any territory within those dominions which is subject to a separate legislature.

14. In relation to the following countries and territories, that is to say, India, the Republic of Ireland, any protectorate, protected state or trust territory within the meaning of the British Nationality Act, 1948, any territory administered under the authority of a country mentioned in subsection (3) of section one of that Act, the Sudan and the New Hebrides, the provisions of this Schedule shall have effect as they have effect in relation to Her Majesty's dominions, and references therein to Her Majesty's dominions shall be construed accordingly.

Table of Statues referred to in this Act

Short Title	Session and Chapter
Parliamentary Papers Act, 1840	3 & 4 Vict c 9
Telegraph Act, 1863	26 & 27 Vict c 112
Law of Libel Amendment Act, 1888	51 & 52 Vict c 64
Local Government (Ireland) Act, 1902	2 Edw 7 c 38
Local Authorities (Admission of the Press to Meetings) Act, 1908	8 Edw 7 c 43
Government of Ireland Act, 1920	10 & 11 Geo 5 c 57
Companies Act, 1948	11 & 12 Geo 6 c 38
British Nationality Act, 1948	11 & 12 Geo 6 c 56
Wireless Telegraphy Act, 1949	12, 13 & 14 Geo 6 c 54

Appendix C

Defamation Act 1996
Ch 31

ARRANGEMENT OF SECTIONS

An Act to amend the law of defamation and to amend the law of limitation with respect to actions for defamation or malicious falsehood. [4th July 1996]

Responsibility for publication

Responsibility for publication

1.—(1) In defamation proceedings a person has a defence if he shows that—
   (a) he was not the author, editor or publisher of the statement complained of,
   (b) he took reasonable care in relation to its publication, and
   (c) he did not know, and had no reason to believe, that what he did
caused or contributed to the publication of a defamatory statement.

(2) For this purpose 'author', 'editor' and 'publisher' have the following meanings, which are further explained in subsection (3)—
'author' means the originator of the statement, but does not include a
person who did not intend that his statement be published at all;
'editor' means a person having editorial or equivalent responsibility
for the content of the statement or the decision to publish it; and
'publisher' means a commercial publisher, that is, a person whose business is issuing material to the public, or a section of the public,
who issues material containing the statement in the course of that
business.

(3) A person shall not be considered the author, editor or publisher of a state-ment if he is only involved—
   (a) in printing, producing, distributing or selling printed material con-
taining the statement;
   (b) in processing, making copies of, distributing, exhibiting or selling
a film or sound recording (as defined in Part I of the Copyright,
Designs and Patents Act 1988) containing the statement;

    (c)   in processing, making copies of, distributing or selling any electronic medium in or on which the statement is recorded, or in operating or providing any equipment, system or service by means of which the statement is retrieved, copied, distributed or made available in electronic form;

    (d)   as the broadcaster of a live programme containing the statement in circumstances in which he has no effective control over the maker of the statement;

    (e)   as the operator of or provider of access to a communications system by means of which the statement is transmitted, or made available, by a person over whom he has no effective control.

In a case not within paragraphs (a) to (e) the court may have regard to those provisions by way of analogy in deciding whether a person is to be considered the author, editor or publisher of a statement.

(4) Employees or agents of an author, editor or publisher are in the same position as their employer or principal to the extent that they are responsible for the content of the statement or the decision to publish it.

(5) In determining for the purposes of this section whether a person took reasonable care, or had reason to believe that what he did caused or contributed to the publication of a defamatory statement, regard shall be had to—

    (a)   the extent of his responsibility for the content of the statement or the decision to publish it,

    (b)   the nature or circumstances of the publication, and

    (c)   the previous conduct or character of the author, editor or publisher.

(6) This section does not apply to any cause of action which arose before the section came into force.

Offer to make amends

Offer to make amends

2.—(1) A person who has published a statement alleged to be defamatory of another may offer to make amends under this section.

(2) The offer may be in relation to the statement generally or in relation to a specific defamatory meaning which the person making the offer accepts that the statement conveys ('a qualified offer').

(3) An offer to make amends—

    (a)   must be in writing,

    (b)   must be expressed to be an offer to make amends under section 2 of the Defamation Act 1996, and

    (c)   must state whether it is a qualified offer and, if so, set out the defamatory meaning in relation to which it is made.

(4) An offer to make amends under this section is an offer—

    (a)   to make a suitable correction of the statement complained of and a sufficient apology to the aggrieved party,

    (b)   to publish the correction and apology in a manner that is reasonable and practicable in the circumstances, and

    (c)   to pay to the aggrieved party such compensation (if any), and such costs, as may be agreed or determined to be payable.

The fact that the offer is accompanied by an offer to take specific steps does not affect the fact that an offer to make amends under this section is an offer to do all the things mentioned in paragraphs (a) to (c).

(5) An offer to make amends under this section may not be made by a person after serving a defence in defamation proceedings brought against him by the aggrieved party in respect of the publication in question.

(6) An offer to make amends under this section may be withdrawn before it is accepted; and a renewal of an offer which has been withdrawn shall be treated as a new offer.

Accepting an offer to make amends

3.—(1) If an offer to make amends under section 2 is accepted by the aggrieved party, the following provisions apply.

(2) The party accepting the offer may not bring or continue defamation proceedings in respect of the publication concerned against the person making the offer, but he is entitled to enforce the offer to make amends, as follows.

(3) If the parties agree on the steps to be taken in fulfilment of the offer, the aggrieved party may apply to the court for an order that the other party fulfil his offer by taking the steps agreed.

(4) If the parties do not agree on the steps to be taken by way of correction, apology and publication, the party who made the offer may take such steps as he thinks appropriate, and may in particular—

    (a)   make the correction and apology by a statement in open court in terms approved by the court, and

    (b)   give an undertaking to the court as to the manner of their publication.

(5) If the parties do not agree on the amount to be paid by way of compensation, it shall be determined by the court on the same principles as damages in defamation proceedings.

The court shall take account of any steps taken in fulfilment of the offer and (so far as not agreed between the parties) of the suitability of the correction, the sufficiency of the apology and whether the manner of their publication was reasonable in the circumstances, and may reduce or increase the amount of compensation accordingly.

(6) If the parties do not agree on the amount to be paid by way of costs, it shall be determined by the court on the same principles as costs awarded in court proceedings.

(7) The acceptance of an offer by one person to make amends does not affect any cause of action against another person in respect of the same publication, subject as follows.

(8) In England and Wales or Northern Ireland, for the purposes of the Civil Liability (Contribution) Act 1978—

    (a)   the amount of compensation paid under the offer shall be treated as paid in bona fide settlement or compromise of the claim; and

    (b)   where another person is liable in respect of the same damage (whether jointly or otherwise), the person whose offer to make amends was accepted is not required to pay by virtue of any con-

tribution under section 1 of that Act a greater amount than the
amount of the compensation payable in pursuance of the offer.

(9) In Scotland—

    (a)   subsection (2) of section 3 of the Law Reform (Miscellaneous Pro-
visions) (Scotland) Act 1940 (right of one joint wrongdoer as respects another to recover contribution towards damages) applies
in relation to compensation paid under an offer to make amends as
it applies in relation to damages in an action to which that section
applies; and

    (b)   where another person is liable in respect of the same damage
(whether jointly or otherwise), the person whose offer to make
amends was accepted is not required to pay by virtue of any contribution under section 3(2) of that Act a greater amount than the
amount of compensation payable in pursuance of the offer.

(10) Proceedings under this section shall be heard and determined without a
jury.

Failure to accept offer to make amends

4.—(1) If an offer to make amends under section 2, duly made and not withdrawn, is not accepted by the aggrieved party, the following provisions apply.

(2) The fact that the offer was made is a defence (subject to subsection (3)) to
defamation proceedings in respect of the publication in question by that party
against the person making the offer.

A qualified offer is only a defence in respect of the meaning to which the
offer related.

(3) There is no such defence if the person by whom the offer was made knew
or had reason to believe that the statement complained of—

    (a)   referred to the aggrieved party or was likely to be understood as
referring to him, and

    (b)   was both false and defamatory of that party;

but it shall be presumed until the contrary is shown that he did not know and had
no reason to believe that was the case.

(4) The person who made the offer need not rely on it by way of defence, but
if he does he may not rely on any other defence.

If the offer was a qualified offer, this applies only in respect of the meaning
to which the offer related.

(5) The offer may be relied on in mitigation of damages whether or not it was
relied on as a defence.

Limitation

Limitation of actions: England and Wales

5.—(1) The Limitation Act 1980 is amended as follows.

(2) For section 4A (time limit for action for libel or slander) substitute—

    '*Time limit for actions for defamation or malicious falsehood*

    4A. The time limit under section 2 of this Act shall not apply to an
action for—

        (a)   libel or slander, or

(b) slander of title, slander of goods or other malicious falsehood,

but no such action shall be brought after the expiration of one year
from the date on which the cause of action accrued.'.

(3) In section 28 (extension of limitation period in case of disability), for
subsection (4A) substitute—

'(4A) If the action is one to which section 4A of this Act applies,
subsection (1) above shall have effect—

(a) in the case of an action for libel or slander, as if for the
words from "at any time" to "occurred)" there were substituted the words "by him at any time before the expiration of
one year from the date on which he ceased to be under a
disability"; and

(b) in the case of an action for slander of title, slander of goods
or other malicious falsehood, as if for the words "six years"
there were substituted the words "one year".'.

(4) For section 32A substitute—

*'Discretionary exclusion of time limit for actions for defamation
or malicious falsehood*

Discretionary exclusion of time limit for actions for defamation or malicious falsehood

32A.—(I) If it appears to the court that it would be equitable to
allow an action to proceed having regard to the degree to which—

(a) the operation of section 4A of this Act prejudices the plaintiff or any person whom he represents, and

(b) any decision of the court under this subsection would prejudice the defendant or any person whom he represents,

the court may direct that that section shall not apply to the action or
shall not apply to any specified cause of action to which the action
relates.

(2) In acting under this section the court shall have regard to all the
circumstances of the case and in particular to—

(a) the length of, and the reasons for, the delay on the part of
the plaintiff;

(b) where the reason or one of the reasons for the delay was
that all or any of the facts relevant to the cause of action did
not become known to the plaintiff until after the end of the
period mentioned in section 4A—

(i) the date on which any such facts did become known to
him, and

(ii) the extent to which he acted promptly and reasonably
once he knew whether or not the facts in question might
be capable of giving rise to an action; and

(c) the extent to which, having regard to the delay, relevant evidence is likely—

(i) to be unavailable, or

(ii) to be less cogent than if the action had been brought

within the period mentioned in section 4A.

(3) In the case of an action for slander of title, slander of goods or other malicious falsehood brought by a personal representative—

(a) the references in subsection (2) above to the plaintiff shall be construed as including the deceased person to whom the cause of action accrued and any previous personal representative of that person; and

(b) nothing in section 28(3) of this Act shall be construed as affecting the court's discretion under this section.

(4) In this section "the court" means the court in which the action has been brought.'.

(5) In section 36(1) (expiry of time limit no bar to equitable relief), for paragraph (aa) substitute—

'(aa) the time limit under section 4A for actions for libel or slander, or for slander of title, slander of goods or other malicious falsehood;'.

(6) The amendments made by this section apply only to causes of action arising after the section comes into force.

Limitation of actions: Northern Ireland

6.—(1) The Limitation (Northern Ireland) Order 1989 is amended as follows:

(2) In Article 6 (time limit: certain actions founded on tort) for paragraph (2) substitute—

'(2) Subject to Article 51, an action for damages for—

(a) libel or slander; or

(b) slander of title, slander of goods or other malicious falsehood,

may not be brought after the expiration of one year from the date on which the cause of action accrued.'.

(3) In Article 48 (extension of time limit), for paragraph (7) substitute—

'(7) Where the action is one to which Article 6(2) applies, paragraph (1) has effect—

(a) in the case of an action for libel and slander, as if for the words from "at any time" to "occurred" there were substituted the words "by him at any time before the expiration of one year from the date on which he ceased to be under a disability"; and

(b) in the case of an action for slander of title, slander of goods or other malicious falsehood, as if for the words "six years" there were substituted the words "one year".'.

(4) For Article 51 substitute—

'Court's power to override time limit: actions for defamation or malicious falsehood

51.—(1) If it appears to the court that it would be equitable to allow an action to proceed having regard to the degree to which—

(a) the provisions of Article 6(2) prejudice the plaintiff or any person whom he represents; and

(b) any decision of the court under this paragraph would prejudice the defendant or any person whom he represents,

the court may direct that those provisions are not to apply to the
action, or are not to apply to any specified cause of action to which
the action relates.

(2) In acting under this Article the court is to have regard to all the
circumstances of the case and in particular to—

(a) the length of, and the reasons for, the delay on the part of
the plaintiff;

(b) in a case where the reason, or one of the reasons, for the
delay was that all or any of the facts relevant to the cause of
action did not become known to the plaintiff until after the
expiration of the period mentioned in Article 6(2)—

    (i) the date on which any such facts did become known to
him, and

    (ii) the extent to which he acted promptly and reasonably
once he knew whether or not the facts in question might
be capable of giving rise to an action; and

(c) the extent to which, having regard to the delay, relevant
evidence is likely—

    (i) to be unavailable, or

    (ii) to be less cogent than if the action had been brought
within the time allowed by Article 6(2).

(3) In the case of an action for slander of title, slander of goods or
other malicious falsehood brought by a personal representative—

(a) the references in paragraph (2) to the plaintiff shall be construed as including the deceased person to whom the cause
of action accrued and any previous personal representative
of that person; and

(b) nothing in Article 48(3) shall be construed as affecting the
court's discretion under this Article.

(4) In this Article "the court" means the court in which the action
has been brought.'.

(5) The amendments made by this section apply only to causes of action
arising after the section comes into force.

The meaning of a statement

Ruling on the meaning of a statement

7. In defamation proceedings the court shall not be asked to rule whether a
statement is arguably capable, as opposed to capable, of bearing a particular
meaning or meanings attributed to it.

Summary disposal of claim

Summary disposal of claim

8.—(1) In defamation proceedings the court may dispose summarily of the
plaintiff's claim in accordance with the following provisions.

(2) The court may dismiss the plaintiff's claim if it appears to the court that
it has no realistic prospect of success and there is no reason why it should be

tried.

(3) The court may give judgment for the plaintiff and grant him summary relief (see section 9) if it appears to the court that there is no defence to the claim which has a realistic prospect of success, and that there is no other reason why the claim should be tried.

Unless the plaintiff asks for summary relief, the court shall not act under this subsection unless it is satisfied that summary relief will adequately compensate him for the wrong he has suffered.

(4) In considering whether a claim should be tried the court shall have regard to—

    (a)   whether all the persons who are or might be defendants in respect of the publication complained of are before the court;

    (b)   whether summary disposal of the claim against another defendant would be inappropriate;

    (c)   the extent to which there is a conflict of evidence;

    (d)   the seriousness of the alleged wrong (as regards the content of the statement and the extent of publication); and

    (e)   whether it is justifiable in the circumstances to proceed to a full trial.

(5) Proceedings under this section shall be heard and determined without a jury.

Meaning of summary relief

9.—(1) For the purposes of section 8 (summary disposal of claim) 'summary relief' means such of the following as may be appropriate—

    (a)   a declaration that the statement was false and defamatory of the plaintiff;

    (b)   an order that the defendant publish or cause to be published a suitable correction and apology;

    (c)   damages not exceeding £10,000 or such other amount as may be prescribed by order of the Lord Chancellor;

    (d)   an order restraining the defendant from publishing or further publishing the matter complained of.

(2) The content of any correction and apology, and the time, manner, form and place of publication, shall be for the parties to agree.

If they cannot agree on the content, the court may direct the defendant to publish or cause to be published a summary of the court's judgment agreed by the parties or settled by the court in accordance with rules of court.

If they cannot agree on the time, manner, form or place of publication, the court may direct the defendant to take such reasonable and practicable steps as the court considers appropriate.

(3) Any order under subsection (1)(c) shall be made by statutory instrument which shall be subject to annulment in pursuance of a resolution of either House of Parliament.

Summary disposal: rules of court

10.—(1) Provision may be made by rules of court as to the summary disposal of the plaintiff's claim in defamation proceedings.

(2) Without prejudice to the generality of that power, provision may be made—

   (a) authorising a party to apply for summary disposal at any stage of the proceedings;

   (b) authorising the court at any stage of the proceedings—

     (i) to treat any application, pleading or other step in the proceedings as an application for summary disposal, or

     (ii) to make an order for summary disposal without any such application;

   (c) as to the time for serving pleadings or taking any other step in the proceedings in a case where there are proceedings for summary disposal;

   (d) requiring the parties to identify any question of law or construction which the court is to be asked to determine in the proceedings;

   (e) as to the nature of any hearing on the question of summary disposal, and in particular—

     (i) authorising the court to order affidavits or witness statements to be prepared for use as evidence at the hearing, and

     (ii) requiring the leave of the court for the calling of oral evidence, or the introduction of new evidence, at the hearing;

   (f) authorising the court to require a defendant to elect, at or before the hearing, whether or not to make an offer to make amends under section 2.

Summary disposal: application to Northern Ireland

11. In their application to Northern Ireland the provisions of sections 8 to 10 (summary disposal of claim) apply only to proceedings in the High Court.

Evidence of convictions

Evidence of convictions

12.—(1) In section 13 of the Civil Evidence Act 1968 (conclusiveness of convictions for purposes of defamation actions), in subsections (1) and (2) for 'a person' substitute 'the plaintiff' and for 'that person' substitute 'he'; and after subsection (2) insert—

'(2A) In the case of an action for libel or slander in which there is more than one plaintiff—

   (a) the references in subsections (1) and (2) above to the plaintiff shall be construed as references to any of the plaintiffs, and

   (b) proof that any of the plaintiffs stands convicted of an offence shall be conclusive evidence that he committed that offence so far as that fact is relevant to any issue arising in relation to his cause of action or that of any other plaintiff.'.

The amendments made by this subsection apply only where the trial of the action begins after this section comes into force.

(2) In section 12 of the Law Reform (Miscellaneous Provisions) (Scotland) Act 1968 (conclusiveness of convictions for purposes of defamation actions), in

subsections (1) and (2) for 'a person' substitute 'the pursuer' and for 'that person' substitute 'he'; and after subsection (2) insert—

> '(2A) In the case of an action for defamation in which there is more than one pursuer—
>
> > (a) the references in subsections (1) and (2) above to the pursuer shall be construed as references to any of the pursuers, and
> >
> > (b) proof that any of the pursuers stands convicted of an offence shall be conclusive evidence that he committed that offence so far as that fact is relevant to any issue arising in relation to his cause of action or that of any other pursuer.'.

The amendments made by this subsection apply only for the purposes of an action begun after this section comes into force, whenever the cause of action arose.

(3) In section 9 of the Civil Evidence Act (Northern Ireland) 1971 (conclusiveness of convictions for purposes of defamation actions), in subsections (1) and (2) for 'a person' substitute 'the plaintiff' and for 'that person' substitute 'he'; and after subsection (2) insert—

> '(2A) In the case of an action for libel or slander in which there is more than one plaintiff—
>
> > (a) the references in subsections (1) and (2) to the plaintiff shall be construed as references to any of the plaintiffs, and
> >
> > (b) proof that any of the plaintiffs stands convicted of an offence shall be conclusive evidence that he committed that offence so far as that fact is relevant to any issue arising in relation to his cause of action or that of any other plaintiff.'.

The amendments made by this subsection apply only where the trial of the action begins after this section comes into force.

Evidence concerning proceedings in Parliament

Evidence concerning proceedings in Parliament

13.—(1) Where the conduct of a person in or in relation to proceedings in Parliament is in issue in defamation proceedings, he may waive for the purposes of those proceedings, so far as concerns him, the protection of any enactment or rule of law which prevents proceedings in Parliament being impeached or questioned in any court or place out of Parliament.

(2) Where a person waives that protection—

> (a) any such enactment or rule of law shall not apply to prevent evidence being given, questions being asked or statements, submissions, comments or findings being made about his conduct, and
>
> (b) none of those things shall be regarded as infringing the privilege of either House of Parliament.

(3) The waiver by one person of that protection does not affect its operation in relation to another person who has not waived it.

(4) Nothing in this section affects any enactment or rule of law so far as it protects a person (including a person who has waived the protection referred to above) from legal liability for words spoken or things done in the course of, or

for the purposes of or incidental to, any proceedings in Parliament.

(5) Without prejudice to the generality of subsection (4), that subsection applies to—

(a) the giving of evidence before either House or a committee;

(b) the presentation or submission of a document to either House or a committee;

(c) the preparation of a document for the purposes of or incidental to the transacting of any such business;

(d) the formulation, making or publication of a document, including a report, by or pursuant to an order of either House or a committee; and

(e) any communication with the Parliamentary Commissioner for Standards or any person having functions in connection with the registration of members' interests.

In this subsection 'a committee' means a committee of either House or a joint committee of both Houses of Parliament.

Statutory privilege

Reports of court proceedings absolutely privileged

14.—(1) A fair and accurate report of proceedings in public before a court to which this section applies, if published contemporaneously with the proceedings, is absolutely privileged.

(2) A report of proceedings which by an order of the court, or as a consequence of any statutory provision, is required to be postponed shall be treated as published contemporaneously if it is published as soon as practicable after publication is permitted.

(3) This section applies to—

(a) any court in the United Kingdom,

(b) the European Court of Justice or any court attached to that court,

(c) the European Court of Human Rights, and

(d) any international criminal tribunal established by the Security Council of the United Nations or by an international agreement to which the United Kingdom is a party.

In paragraph (a) 'court' includes any tribunal or body exercising the judicial power of the State.

(4) In section 8(6) of the Rehabilitation of Offenders Act 1974 and in Article 9(6) of the Rehabilitation of Offenders (Northern Ireland) Order 1978 (defamation actions: reports of court proceedings), for 'section 3 of the Law of Libel Amendment Act 1888' substitute 'section 14 of the Defamation Act 1996'.

Reports, &c protected by qualified privilege

15.—(1) The publication of any report or other statement mentioned in Schedule 1 to this Act is privileged unless the publication is shown to be made with malice, subject as follows.

(2) In defamation proceedings in respect of the publication of a report or other statement mentioned in Part II of that Schedule, there is no defence under

this section if the plaintiff shows that the defendant—

(a) was requested by him to publish in a suitable manner a reasonable letter or statement by way of explanation or contradiction, and

(b) refused or neglected to do so.

For this purpose 'in a suitable manner' means in the same manner as the publication complained of or in a manner that is adequate and reasonable in the circumstances.

(3) This section does not apply to the publication to the public, or a section of the public, of matter which is not of public concern and the publication of which is not for the public benefit.

(4) Nothing in this section shall be construed—

(a) as protecting the publication of matter the publication of which is prohibited by law, or

(b) as limiting or abridging any privilege subsisting apart from this section.

Supplementary provisions

Repeals

16. The enactments specified in Schedule 2 are repealed to the extent specified.

Interpretation

17.—(1) In this Act—

'publication' and 'publish', in relation to a statement, have the meaning they have for the purposes of the law of defamation generally, but 'publisher' is specially defined for the purposes of section l;

'statement' means words, pictures, visual images, gestures or any other method of signifying meaning; and

'statutory provision' means—

(a) a provision contained in an Act or in subordinate legislation within the meaning of the Interpretation Act 1978, or

(b) a statutory provision within the meaning given by section 1(f) of the Interpretation Act (Northern Ireland) 1954.

(2) In this Act as it applies to proceedings in Scotland—

'costs' means expenses; and

'plaintiff' and 'defendant' mean pursuer and defender.

General provisions

Extent

18.—(1) The following provisions of this Act extend to England and Wales—

section 1 (responsibility for publication),

sections 2 to 4 (offer to make amends), except section 3(9),

section 5 (time limit for actions for defamation or malicious falsehood),

section 7 (ruling on the meaning of a statement),

sections 8 to 10 (summary disposal of claim),

section 12(1) (evidence of convictions),

section 13 (evidence concerning proceedings in Parliament),

sections 14 and 15 and Schedule 1 (statutory privilege),

section 16 and Schedule 2 (repeals) so far as relating to enactments extending to England and Wales,

section 17(1) (interpretation),

this subsection,

section 19 (commencement) so far as relating to provisions which extend to England and Wales, and

section 20 (short title and saving).

(2) The following provisions of this Act extend to Scotland—

section 1 (responsibility for publication),

sections 2 to 4 (offer to make amends), except section 3(8),

section 12(2) (evidence of convictions),

section 13 (evidence concerning proceedings in Parliament),

sections 14 and 15 and Schedule 1 (statutory privilege),

section 16 and Schedule 2 (repeals) so far as relating to enactments extending to Scotland,

section 17 (interpretation),

this subsection,

section 19 (commencement) so far as relating to provisions which extend to Scotland, and

section 20 (short title and saving).

(3) The following provisions of this Act extend to Northern Ireland—

section 1 (responsibility for publication),

sections 2 to 4 (offer to make amends), except section 3(9),

section 6 (time limit for actions for defamation or malicious falsehood),

section 7 (ruling on the meaning of a statement),

sections 8 to 11 (summary disposal of claim),

section 12(3) (evidence of convictions),

section 13 (evidence concerning proceedings in Parliament),

sections 14 and 15 and Schedule 1 (statutory privilege),

section 16 and Schedule 2 (repeals) so far as relating to enactments extending to Northern Ireland,

section 17(1) (interpretation),

this subsection,

section 19 (commencement) so far as relating to provisions which extend to Northern Ireland, and

section 20 (short title and saving).

Commencement

19.—(1) Sections 18 to 20 (extent, commencement and other general provisions) come into force on Royal Assent.

(2) The following provisions of this Act come into force at the end of the period of two months beginning with the day on which this Act is passed—

section 1 (responsibility for publication),

sections 5 and 6 (time limit for actions for defamation or malicious falsehood),

section 12 (evidence of convictions),

section 13 (evidence concerning proceedings in Parliament),

section 16 and the repeals in Schedule 2, so far as consequential on the above provisions, and

section 17 (interpretation), so far as relating to the above provisions.

(3) The provisions of this Act otherwise come into force on such day as may be appointed—

(a)   for England and Wales or Northern Ireland, by order of the Lord Chancellor, or

(b)   for Scotland, by order of the Secretary of State,

and different days may be appointed for different purposes.

(4) Any such order shall be made by statutory instrument and may contain such transitional provisions as appear to the Lord Chancellor or Secretary of State to be appropriate.

Short title and saving

20.—(1) This Act may be cited as the Defamation Act 1996.

(2) Nothing in this Act affects the law relating to criminal libel.

SCHEDULES

Section 15

SCHEDULE 1

QUALIFIED PRIVILEGE

PART I

STATEMENTS HAVING QUALIFIED PRIVILEGE WITHOUT EXPLANATION OR CONTRADICTION

1. A fair and accurate report of proceedings in public of a legislature any-where in the world.

2. A fair and accurate report of proceedings in public before a court any-where in the world.

3. A fair and accurate report of proceedings in public of a person appointed to hold a public inquiry by a government or legislature anywhere in the world.

4. A fair and accurate report of proceedings in public anywhere in the world of an international organisation or an international conference.

5. A fair and accurate copy of or extract from any register or other document required by law to be open to public inspection.

6. A notice or advertisement published by or on the authority of a court, or of a judge or officer of a court, anywhere in the world.

7. A fair and accurate copy of or extract from matter published by or on the authority of a government or legislature anywhere in the world.

8. A fair and accurate copy of or extract from matter published anywhere in the world by an international organisation or an international conference.

PART II

STATEMENTS PRIVILEGED SUBJECT TO EXPLANATION OR CONTRADICTION

9.—(1) A fair and accurate copy of or extract from a notice or other matter issued for the information of the public by or on behalf of—

(a) a legislature in any member State or the European Parliament;

(b) the government of any member State, or any authority performing governmental functions in any member State or part of a member State, or the European Commission;

(c) an international organisation or international conference.

(2) In this paragraph 'governmental functions' includes police functions.

10. A fair and accurate copy of or extract from a document made available by a court in any member State or the European Court of Justice (or any court attached to that court), or by a judge or officer of any such court.

11.—(1) A fair and accurate report of proceedings at any public meeting or sitting in the United Kingdom of—

(a) a local authority or local authority committee;

(b) a justice or justices of the peace acting otherwise than as a court exercising judicial authority;

(c) a commission, tribunal, committee or person appointed for the purposes of any inquiry by any statutory provision, by Her Majesty or by a Minister of the Crown or a Northern Ireland Department;

(d) a person appointed by a local authority to hold a local inquiry in pursuance of any statutory provision;

(e) any other tribunal, board, committee or body constituted by or under, and exercising functions under, any statutory provision.

(2) In sub-paragraph (1)(a)—

'local authority' means—

(a) in relation to England and Wales, a principal council within the meaning of the Local Government Act 1972, any body falling within any paragraph of section 100J(1) of that Act or an authority or body to which the Public Bodies (Admission to Meetings) Act 1960 applies,

(b) in relation to Scotland, a council constituted under section 2 of the Local Government etc. (Scotland) Act 1994 or an authority or body to which the Public Bodies (Admission to Meetings) Act 1960 applies,

(c) in relation to Northern Ireland, any authority or body to which sections 23 to 27 of the Local Government Act (Northern Ireland) 1972 apply; and

'local authority committee' means any committee of a local authority or of local authorities, and includes—

(a) any committee or sub-committee in relation to which sections 100A to 100D of the Local Government Act 1972 apply by virtue of section 100E of that Act (whether or not also by virtue of section 100J of that Act), and

(b) any committee or sub-committee in relation to which sections 50A to 50D of the Local Government (Scotland) Act 1973 apply by virtue of section 50E of that Act.

(3) A fair and accurate report of any corresponding proceedings in any of the Channel Islands or the Isle of Man or in another member State.

12.—(1) A fair and accurate report of proceedings at any public meeting held in a member State.

(2) In this paragraph a 'public meeting' means a meeting bona fide and lawfully held for a lawful purpose and for the furtherance or discussion of a matter of public concern, whether admission to the meeting is general or restricted.

13.—(1) A fair and accurate report of proceedings at a general meeting of a UK public company.

(2) A fair and accurate copy of or extract from any document circulated to members of a UK public company—

(a) by or with the authority of the board of directors of the company,

(b) by the auditors of the company, or

(c) by any member of the company in pursuance of a right conferred by any statutory provision.

(3) A fair and accurate copy of or extract from any document circulated to members of a UK public company which relates to the appointment, resignation, retirement or dismissal of directors of the company.

(4) In this paragraph 'UK public company' means—

(a) a public company within the meaning of section 1(3) of the Companies Act 1985 or Article 12(3) of the Companies (Northern Ireland) Order 1986, or

(b) a body corporate incorporated by or registered under any other statutory provision, or by Royal Charter, or formed in pursuance of letters patent.

(5) A fair and accurate report of proceedings at any corresponding meeting of, or copy of or extract from any corresponding document circulated to members of, a public company formed under the law of any of the Channel Islands or the Isle of Man or of another member State.

14. A fair and accurate report of any finding or decision of any of the following descriptions of association, formed in the United Kingdom or another member State, or of any committee or governing body of such an association—

(a) an association formed for the purpose of promoting or encouraging the exercise of or interest in any art, science, religion or learning, and empowered by its constitution to exercise control over or adjudicate on matters of interest or concern to the association, or the actions or conduct of any person subject to such control or adjudication;

(b) an association formed for the purpose of promoting or safeguarding the interests of any trade, business, industry or profession, or of the persons carrying on or engaged in any trade, business, industry or profession, and empowered by its constitution to exercise control over or adjudicate upon matters connected with that trade, business, industry or profession, or the actions or conduct of those persons;

(c) an association formed for the purpose of promoting or safeguarding the interests of a game, sport or pastime to the playing or exercise of which members of the public are invited or admitted, and empowered by its constitution to exercise control over or adjudicate upon persons connected with or taking part in the game, sport or pastime;

(d) an association formed for the purpose of promoting charitable objects or other objects beneficial to the community and empowered by its constitution to exercise control over or to adjudicate on matters of interest or concern to the association, or the actions or conduct of any person subject to such control or adjudication.

15.—(1) A fair and accurate report of, or copy of or extract from, any adjudication, report, statement or notice issued by a body, officer or other person designated for the purposes of this paragraph—

(a) for England and Wales or Northern Ireland, by order of the Lord Chancellor, and

(b) for Scotland, by order of the Secretary of State.

(2) An order under this paragraph shall be made by statutory instrument which shall be subject to annulment in pursuance of a resolution of either House of Parliament.

PART III

SUPPLEMENTARY PROVISIONS

16.—(1) In this Schedule—

'court' includes any tribunal or body exercising the judicial power of the State;

'international conference' means a conference attended by representatives of two or more governments;

'international organisation' means an organisation of which two or more governments are members, and includes any committee or other subordinate body of such an organisation; and

'legislature' includes a local legislature.

(2) References in this Schedule to a member State include any European dependent territory of a member State.

(3) In paragraphs 2 and 6 'court' includes—

(a) the European Court of Justice (or any court attached to that court) and the Court of Auditors of the European Communities,

(b) the European Court of Human Rights,

(c) any international criminal tribunal established by the Security Council of the United Nations or by an international agreement to which the United Kingdom is a party, and

(d) the International Court of Justice and any other judicial or arbitral tribunal deciding matters in dispute between States.

(4) In paragraphs 1, 3 and 7 'legislature' includes the European Parliament.

17.—(1) Provision may be made by order identifying—

　　(a) for the purposes of paragraph 11, the corresponding proceedings referred to in sub-paragraph (3);

　　(b) for the purposes of paragraph 13, the corresponding meetings and documents referred to in sub-paragraph (5).

(2) An order under this paragraph may be made—

　　(a) for England and Wales or Northern Ireland, by the Lord Chancellor, and

　　(b) for Scotland, by the Secretary of State.

(3) An order under this paragraph shall be made by statutory instrument which shall be subject to annulment in pursuance of a resolution of either House of Parliament.

Section 16

SCHEDULE 2

REPEALS

Chapter	Short title	Extent of repeal
1888 c 64	Law of Libel Amendment Act 1888	Section 3
1952 c 66	Defamation Act 1952	Section 4. Sections 7, 8 and 9(2) and (3). Section 16(2) and (3). The Schedule
1955 c 20	Revision of the Army and Air Force Acts (Transitional Provisions) Act 1955	In Schedule 2, the entry relating to the Defamation Act 1952
1955 c 11 (NI)	Defamation Act (Northern Ireland) 1955	Section 4. Sections 7, 8 and 9(2) and (3). Section 14(2). The Schedule
1972 c 9 (NI)	Local Government Act (Northern Ireland) 1972	In Schedule 8, paragraph 12

1981 c 49	Contempt of Court Act 1981	In section 4(3), the words 'and of section 3 of the Law of Libel Amendment Act 1888 (privilege)'
1981 c 61	British Nationality Act 1981	In Schedule 7, the entries relating to the Defamation Act 1952 and the Defamation Act (Northern Ireland) 1955
1985 c 43	Local Government (Access to Information) Act 1985.	In Schedule 2, paragraphs 2 and 3
1985 c 61	Administration of Justice Act 1985	Section 57
SI 1986/594 (NI)	Education and Libraries (Northern Ireland) Order 1986	Article 97(2)
1990 c 42	Broadcasting Act 1990	Section 166(3). In Schedule 20, paragraphs 2 and 3

Appendix D

Chart of Highest and Lowest Libel
Damages Awards in Years 1986–1996

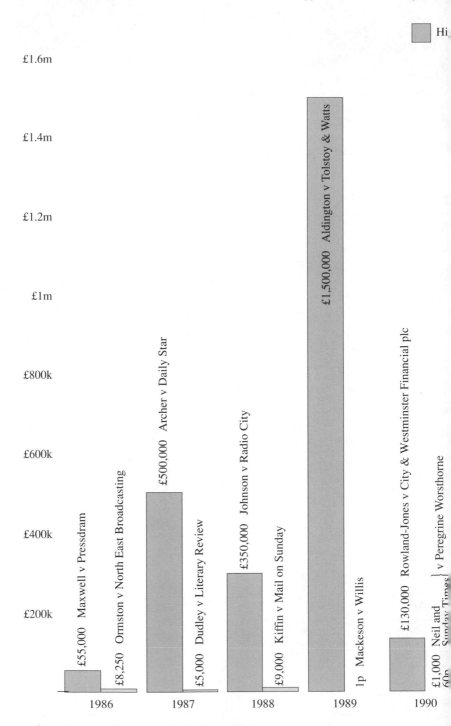

Appendix D. Chart of highest an

Hi

£1.6m

£1.4m

£1.2m

£1m

£800k

£600k

£400k

£200k

£55,000 Maxwell v Pressdram

£8,250 Ormston v North East Broadcasting

£500,000 Archer v Daily Star

£5,000 Dudley v Literary Review

£350,000 Johnson v Radio City

£9,000 Kiffin v Mail on Sunday

£1,500,000 Aldington v Tolstoy & Watts

1p Mackeson v Willis

£130,000 Rowland-Jones v City & Westminster Financial plc

} v Peregrine Worsthorne

£1,000 Neil and Sunday Times
60p

1986   1987   1988   1989   1990

bel damages awards in years 1986 to 1996

d 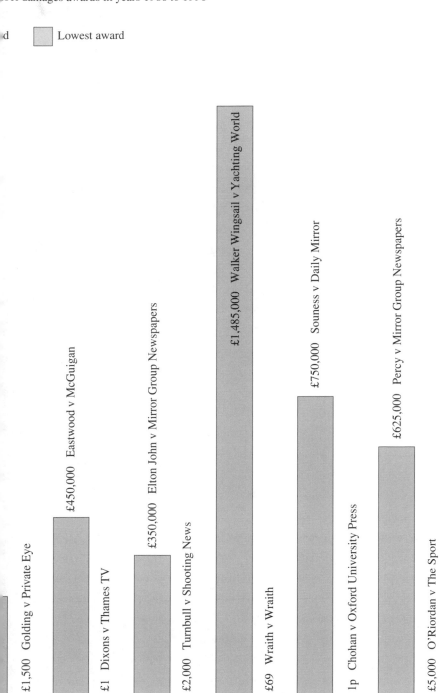 Lowest award

Highest award

£1,485,000 Walker Wingsail v Yachting World

£750,000 Souness v Daily Mirror

£625,000 Percy v Mirror Group Newspapers

£450,000 Eastwood v McGuigan

£350,000 Elton John v Mirror Group Newspapers

£1,500 Golding v Private Eye

£1 Dixons v Thames TV

£2,000 Turnbull v Shooting News

£69 Wraith v Wraith

1p Chohan v Oxford University Press

£5,000 O'Riordan v The Sport

1991 1992 1993 1994 1995 1996

Index